A SENIOR'S GUIDE FOR LIVING WELL, AND DYING WELL

Conversations That Matter

A SENIOR'S GUIDE FOR LIVING WELL, AND DYING WELL

Conversations That Matter

A. Stuart Hanson, MD

Illustrations by Carolyn Papke

Wolfe Lake Press
ISBN 978-1-7923-2528-1

PRINTED IN THE UNITED STATES OF AMERICA

For

Sue Larson

David Litsey

and

Robert Ramsey

CONTENTS

PART THREE: Our Legacies

ACKNOWLEDGMENTS

The contributors to this book include residents of a senior independent-living facility called Parkshore Apartments in St. Louis Park, a suburb of Minneapolis, Minnesota. The 13-story apartment building has 220 units and about 280 residents 55 and older. Most residents are in their 70s, 80s, and 90s. The *Conversations That Matter* guide group includes Sue Larson, Shelby Andress, Lee Wilson, Joyce Pederson, David Litsey, Audrey Rees, Carolyn Papke, Ron Allen, and Robert Ramsey.

Other contributors include Craig Litsey, a lawyer and financial planner; Carol Stephens, a psychologist who contributed to the "What's Important to Me" chapter; Lisa Bolin, a sleep disorders and pulmonary physician; Marion Franz, a dietetic educator; Rachael Freed, a family letters presenter; and Tom Fraser, JD, a checklist for organizing important documents.

Resources have been received from The National Sleep Foundation, The National Heart, Lung, and Blood Institute, Harvard Medical Center, Jewish Family Services of Minneapolis, AAA Foundation for Traffic Safety, US Centers for Disease Control and Prevention, National Center for Injury Prevention and Control, State of Minnesota Attorney General's Guide on Probate and Planning, the Twin Cities Medical Society and its Honoring Choices initiative, The Minnesota Medical Association POLST form, and The National End-of-Life Doula Alliance.

We wish to thank Anne Czarniecki for her superb talents in editing these chapters and to Rachel Holscher and Ann Sudmeier at Bookmobile for the design and printing of this guide.

We are grateful for all the resources the presenters have made available to us and for all the sources available from public libraries and the internet. We realize this workbook is incomplete in areas that may be of specific interest to the reader, and we apologize for any issues of importance we have not addressed.

INTRODUCTION

This book is intended to give seniors a broad overview of the critical issues we are now or will be facing as we age. It can be hard to discuss later-in-life issues such as declining heath, dwindling finances, and how we want to die. We need to get past our personal barriers and intentionally make the important decisions for our lives.

In 2015 a small group of interested residents at our senior independent-living facility began planning an initiative to address end-of-life issues that many of us had faced with our spouses and that all of us would be personally facing at some time in the future.

We started building awareness by promoting a community reading of Atul Gawande's book, *Being Mortal: Medicine and What Matters in the End* and by holding book-discussion groups. We also aired the PBS Frontline Television video, "Being Mortal," where Dr. Atul Gawande interviews dying patients and their physicians. We found that the book and video opened up new informal conversations among members of the community. We found that there was genuine interest in learning more about dying well, but also significant interest in living well. We held monthly programs related to the end of life over the remaining months of the year.

The next year the guiding group planned a series of programs on living well. Our building has new residents joining the community during most months of the year. After the first two years, we felt we needed to repeat the cycle. We are now over four years into a vital program that continues to gain momentum.

In reviewing what we have accomplished, we found one need that was not being met. There are many books, pamphlets, and other materials addressing the subjects we were covering. However, there was no practical workbook that put these important issues, the necessary forms, and critical information in one place. We felt that participants and their families should be able to easily access this information when needed.

The book has three main sections which are: aging well, healthcare issues, and our legacies.

The first section covers living well as we age. Subjects include thinking ahead and finding purpose in retirement. Where should we live, how can we plan the lifestyle we desire, and how can we anticipate potential crises? Mobility issues eventually affect all of us: when should we stop driving as our faculties change, and how do we keep physically and mentally active? We cover depression and anxieties that often coincide and limit an individual's engagement with others and their community. And we address the scams and fraudulent activities perpetrated on seniors.

The second section relates to healthcare and end-of-life issues. Here we cover our aging physical and mental changes. We describe the capabilities and limitations of complex healthcare interventions. We explain palliative and hospice care and medical-aids-in-dying. It is essential to document our informed wishes on how we want to be treated medically.

In the third section we try to make it simple and easy to overcome the resistance many of us have to writing down our thoughts and filling out forms and documents. We discuss healthcare and financial agents who can take over when we are unable to make our own decisions. Many of us also want to leave a legacy beyond property. A family letter sharing the values you wish the family to continue can be very meaningful after you are gone.

We are all different individuals and approach these issues from individual points of view. Making our wishes known in writing is important, but having conversations with the people close to us is equally important. Our family, close friends, caregivers, and clergy all will relate to you better when they are included in conversations about your wishes at the end of life.

The experiences of the *Conversations That Matter* guide group have impacted all of us. We wish to document these experiences with this guidebook in the hope that our later years will be more intentional and satisfying. You are encouraged to write notes in this workbook.

PART ONE

Aging Well

→ thinking ahead →

GETTING STARTED

As we age we begin to shift our priorities. Some, but sadly, not all, of us began in our fifties to seriously consider our future and retirement. We are entering the last half of our expected lives. Our concerns about careers, raising children, and leisure-time activities are changing. The prospect of retirement gets closer each year. Caring for house and yard can become more onerous. The more candid we are about our long-term needs, wishes, and desires, the more enjoyable and satisfying our elder years can be. These are the conversations that matter.

Where shall we live? Many of us would like to stay in our long-term homes. But the cost and effort of keeping up a house and yard, or staying on the farm or an acreage, make us consider our aging physical and mental capacities. The energy we have in our sixties and seventies is not going to be the same in our eighties and nineties. Planning ahead and considering our future health and wealth, while we are able, can be fulfilling and save a lot of headaches and dissatisfaction when an emergency move is required.

Do we want to move to a warmer climate? The options are many. Real estate developers are ready with enticing marketing materials. They would like to take our life savings as a down payment for what seems like gracious living and security in senior communities. The opportunities can be confusing and often lead to putting off realistic decisions until an emergency develops. While not every individual has multiple choices, the following example is useful.

Joan and Steve were in their mid-sixties. They downsized from a single-family home where they raised their children to a three-level townhouse in the same Midwestern city. They enjoyed being close to the city center where they could walk to stores, parks, entertainment, and sporting events. A university was within biking distance. They wanted to keep their townhouse as long as they could.

As they reached their late seventies, one of them developed arthritis, which led to a joint replacement. The townhouse stairs became difficult to manage. It was clear they needed to live in a one-floor unit. They looked ahead and felt they could manage a market-rate apartment for several years, but they were not interested in making further moves during the time they had left. Senior apartments with interesting activities sounded appealing. Their own parents and other family members had had positive experiences in their late years living independently in a senior building near where Steve had worked. The waiting list was long, but they were not in a crisis. They were offered a suitable apartment after about a year. Their adult children, who lived in other parts of the country, thought they were getting ahead of themselves. Their daughter asked, "You're not ready to move into the building where Grandma lived, are you?" After further family discussion everyone's questions were resolved.

Joan and Steve made the move on their own terms before a crisis forced them to move. As with the many issues in life, planning ahead can make a major difference in creating an enjoyable and satisfying lifestyle as we age. Even if you expect to live to 100, you still need a plan.

QUESTIONS TO CONSIDER:

- *Where in the country (or world) do I want to live?*

- *What type of housing do I want?*

- *Will I be close to family and friends?*

- *Will I be able to get where I want to go?*

- *What can I afford?*

- *Will I have easy access to health care?*

- *Will I have convenient access to groceries and shops?*

- *Will I have access to parks and nature?*

- *Where will I walk and exercise?*

- *What other issues do I have?*

FINDING PURPOSE IN RETIREMENT

It is said there are three main decisions that adults make in life. First, what do we want to do for work? Most of us need to gain some sustainable employment when we leave our childhood homes. We might delay work by pursuing education, training, or travel, but eventually most of us need to find work, meaningful and fulfilling work if possible.

The second big decision is whether to get married and to whom. Choosing a compatible partner as a young adult can be a challenge.

The third big decision is when to retire and what to do without our job status. Where do we live when work no longer requires us to live in a specific location? Will we be able to maintain relationships with family and friends? Will retirement funds be sufficient to maintain a desirable lifestyle? Will there be enough activities to occupy our newly available time? Will our activities be meaningful, fulfilling?

There are many books that address these questions. The one our team has found useful is *Claiming Your Place at the Fire* by Richard Lieder and David Shapiro. It focuses on the second half of life. Leider and Shapiro list four questions to consider as we grow into elderhood. Our work group has condensed and modified their work to fit our later-in-life needs.

1. Who am I? (What are my life stories? What is my place in the extended arc of my family's storyline?)
2. Where do I belong? (What is my community? Who are my family and friends?)

3. What do I care about? (What activities are meaningful? What wisdom do I have to share?)
4. What is my life purpose? (What is my calling? What is my legacy?)

We need to spend time on these significant questions. Living intentionally requires us to think deeply about ourselves and why we are here. Having a life plan can make each day more meaningful. Answering these questions can become the foundation of living well into our later years. We can continue to grow as we age. Curiosity can make our lives interesting and challenging. Melding lifelong curiosity and living with a purpose can make our lives meaningful. And we can become a valuable resource for family, friends, our community, and any organization with which we are affiliated. That's a recipe for pleasure and satisfaction in living.

QUESTIONS TO CONSIDER:

- *What are the important events and stories of my life?*

- *What place or places are important for me?*

- *What do I care about?*

- *What is my purpose?*

- *What values can I share with my family?*

KEEPING HEALTHY

Many of us entering elderhood bring with us a long list of ailments that may limit our physical activity. I claim middle age goes from age forty to eighty. When I was eighty, I admitted that I had entered a new phase of my life. Arthritis had limited my active lifestyle and I saw my energy level and stamina diminishing. However, I was able to remain active by walking, biking, working out with weights, and gardening.

Experts say we should stay physically active at every age and with most physical conditions. Some choose to hire a personal trainer for an exercise program and help with motivation. Many of us know what we like to do and what we should be doing to keep our bodies in shape. We can exercise with a friend or a group to stay motivated. Staying physically fit is so important to ease us into elderhood gently. Many seniors can reduce their need for medications and other treatments by remaining physically active. Recent studies suggest there are nerve changes with exercise along with muscle and bone preservation. The neurological effects of exercise may also prevent memory loss as we age. Exercise is a key ingredient to good senior health.

Nutrition is another important aspect of healthy aging. "You are what you eat" is a saying that we have heard since childhood. We should modify that to say, "You are what you eat and don't burn up." One of America's major health problems is obesity and being overweight has its own health consequences. Overweight people are more likely to have chronic diseases such as diabetes, hypertension, heart disease, and arthritis. You may ask, How does your weight affect your arthritis? The simple answer is our joints wear out as we age. Obese individuals put more strain on their larger joints, primarily on hips and knees. Over the years this wear and tear to weight-bearing joints leads to the increased likelihood of surgical replacement.

What does the knowledge of nutrition and exercise tell us about what we should be doing as we age? First, regular exercise is key. A 15 to 30 minute walk 3 to 4 times each week is a good start. If walking is difficult due to arthritis or joint or postural deformity, exercise in a swimming pool. Exercising with a friend or in a group is a good way to keep it up for the long term. Keeping a schedule with other people makes it easier to show up on bad-weather days or when we lack personal motivation.

Not all of us have access to fresh vegetables and fruits that we know are healthy. We need a minimum of five fruit and vegetable servings each day and more is better. Access to fresh produce can be limited by where we live, the season of the year, and by the cost. Pre-cooked meals are convenient, but are often less nutritious than meals made at home or by a restaurant. We need to reduce our portion size as we age.

Some of us take vitamins and supplements. A daily multiple vitamin is unlikely to hurt us, but can complicate other prescribed medications. Any supplements should be discussed with your primary healthcare provider.

QUESTIONS TO CONSIDER:

- *What exercise can I do 3–4 times a week?*

- *Is my diet right for me?*

- *Do I eat enough and not too much?*

Community Engagement

ENGAGING WITH OUR COMMUNITY

Our health and longevity can be enhanced by being active—both physically, emotionally, and mentally. Many of us find helping others to be personally rewarding and satisfying. Consider continuing volunteer activities that you started while still working. Or look for a new way to contribute. We want to find an enjoyable way to be of service to others.

If you do not need a regular income, there are many options. But if you need some additional income beyond social security and other retirement plans, consider reducing your hours and keeping your regular job. Or find a new part-time job that meets your needs and frees up some time for other enjoyable and worthwhile activities.

Many of us are already connected to a church, synagogue, mosque, or temple. Most religious communities are supported by members who volunteer for committees, programs, and office or maintenance services. Consider involving yourself with civic organizations, service clubs, or fraternal organizations.

Political organizations are always looking for volunteers, especially in election years. Volunteer to be an election judge. Most communities are looking for adults from major parties to train and to serve during elections. Election days can be long, but you earn the satisfaction of participating in our government's most fundamental function.

There are numerous opportunities to get involved no matter where we live. The many choices can lead us to become overextended and to burnout. Make two lists. List your current activities. Then list other opportunities or interests you would like to try. Perhaps you might like to volunteer at charities you support. Take the time to think about where you want to offer your talents. Make a plan so you can find focus and fulfillment.

CONSIDERATIONS:

- Make a list of your current activities (work, volunteer, entertainment, sports, etc.).

- Make a list of things you would like to do (travel, new sport, new volunteer activities, etc.).

- Draw from both lists to make a realistic list for yourself.

DRIVING

We like our freedom. The automobile is integral to our sense of freedom as we age. We may have been safe and excellent drivers in our younger years, but as we age our faculties and skills are diminished. Many of us resist giving up our car. How do we know when we are a danger to ourselves and to others? When is it time to call it quits? In this chapter we will give some helpful guidelines.

Physical changes in our bodies can make driving less safe as we age. Our vision is an obvious issue. The clouding of our eye lenses, due to cataracts, causes glare, especially at night. Cataract surgery can help, but it's not perfect. There is also macular degeneration or the reduction of central vision. Treatment can slow vision loss, but again, it is not totally corrective. Aging can cause us difficulty with distant, close, peripheral, and color vision, and depth perception.

There is also the problem of the medications we take. Drugs for heart, blood pressure, and diabetes can interfere with our ability to safely operate a vehicle. Alcohol consumption compounds the problem. Arthritis or numbness can make manipulating foot or hand controls more difficult. Hearing loss makes it hard to localize noise in your surroundings. Reaction times are slower as we age. Driving more slowly does not always solve the problem. In fact, driving more slowly than the traffic around us may be more dangerous.

Ellen was in her eighties when her husband died. He had done most of the driving up to that point. She kept their car and drove it for short trips in her community. When her adult children began talking to her about using other forms of transportation, she said, "I turn right most of the time, and I never go where I haven't been before." As she and her friends became older, she had become their chauffeur for several years. She never had an accident, and nobody reported any near misses. Then one day she became lost after she dropped off her last passenger. She had to seek assistance to get back on a street she recognized. She was embarrassed to tell her family what had happened, but realized how vulnerable she was. She accepted the fact that it was time to let others do the driving. She gave the car to her granddaughter and signed up for Metro Mobility.

The point of this story is: *DON'T WAIT FOR A CRISIS.* Leave the driving to others before you get into an accident.

"But how do I know when I am not safe on the road? I've been driving for sixty years." State departments of transportation do screening vision tests with drivers' license renewals. Some states will offer or require a behind-the-wheel driving test. The American Automobile Association (AAA) provides driver-education sessions and testing. Many healthcare organizations offer driver assessment and education through their occupational-therapy departments. Most communities have resources to help seniors determine when it is time to reduce or to give up driving.

The AAA is an excellent resource. Safe transportation is their business, and the AAA Foundation for Traffic Safety is a good place to start. They have a self-rating form for drivers sixty-five and over. We have modified it for this guide with AAA permission. Try to honestly answer all the questions and show your answers to your family.

How does one sign ↑ for metro Mobility?
Are there requirements for " "

	Always or Almost Always	Some- times	Never or Almost Never
1. I signal and check to the rear when I change lanes.			
2. I wear a seat belt.			
3. I try to stay informed on changes in driving and highway laws and techniques.			
4. Intersections bother me because there is so much to watch from all directions.			
5. I find it difficult to decide when to merge with traffic on a busy interstate highway.			
6. I think I am slower than I used to be in reacting to dangerous driving conditions.			
7. When I am upset, it affects my driving.			
8. My thoughts wander when I drive.			
9. Traffic situations make me angry.			
10. I get regular eye exams to keep my vision sharp.			
11. I check with my doctor or pharmacist about how my medications affect my driving ability.			
12. I try to stay informed of current information about health wellness habits.			
13. My children, or other family members or friends have expressed concern about my driving ability.			
14. How many traffic tickets, warnings, or discussions with law enforcement officers have you had in the last two years?			
15. How many collisions have you had during the last two years?			

Look over your answers and give yourself an assessment by answering this question: DOES MY DRIVING ENDANGER ME OR OTHERS AROUND ME?

In metropolitan ares you can find public buses, trains, and taxi services. Volunteer drivers are available in some communities. Some organizations and religious groups provide transportation services. Senior communities may provide shuttle services. Friends and relatives often fill in. Lyft and Uber have revolutionized the personal-ride industry. All the above options require some pre-trip planning, but loss of spontaneity can be worth the feeling of personal safety. Try out several of the alternatives. Change is stressful, but practice makes perfect.

Think about the expense involved in driving your car. One of the exercises we find useful is to estimate the cost of keeping a private automobile as opposed to using personal-ride services like a taxi or a ride service.

ORIGINAL COST of MY CAR _____

CURRENT VALUE _____

MY CURRENT ANNUAL AUTO COSTS

Insurance per year _____

Gas per month _____ × 12 _____

Parking fees/mo _____ × 12 _____

Maintenance per year _____
   (incl. tires, oil change, etc.)

Garage rental/month _____ × 12 _____
   (If applicable)

Lease payments/mo _____ × 12 _____
   (If applicable)

Original vehicle cost divided by 10 (annual allocation) _____

ESTIMATED ANNUAL COST _____

THE COST OF ALTERNATIVE TRANSPORTATION

Number of trips/month. _____ × 12 _____

Average cost /trip. _____

ESTIMATED COST OF ALTERNATIVE TRANSPORTATION
   (Number of trips × avg. cost) _____

DIFFERENCE BETWEEN KEEPING YOUR CAR
   AND USING ALTERNATIVE TRANSPORTATION _____
     (Auto annual cost minus alternative transportation cost)

Gradually trying out other forms of transportation will make you familiar with what is available in your community. Try taking a bus, taxi, or Uber/ Lyft with a friend or family member to an event and use this form to add up your current vehicle costs and compare it to what you might spend on alternate transportation.

QUESTIONS TO CONSIDER:

- *Am I concerned about my responses to any of the driving questions?*

- *Do I understand why my family is concerned about my driving?*

- *Do I sometimes get confused when I drive?*

- *Do I always take appropriate safety measures when I drive?*

- *Do I know how much my vehicle costs per year?*

- *Have I tried alternate forms of transportation?*

SLEEPING

Sleep is one of the essential functions of living. Without sleep humans function erratically. With adequate sleep humans function more optimally. But what is adequate sleep? Seniors' sleep patterns are different from children and younger adults. These differences are important to understand and affect the length and quality of our sleep as we age.

A lack of quality sleep can lead to mental changes including problems with memory, difficulty concentrating, solving problems, and just staying alert. There are medical conditions associated with lack of sleep. Heart disease, diabetes, weight gain, high blood pressure, stroke, and depression have all been associated with inadequate sleep. Inadequate sleep is a major problem for a large portion of the US adult population. Sleepy drivers cause thousands of motor vehicle crashes each year.

The normal sleep characteristics have been studied extensively. Sleep scientists identify five stages by measuring brain-wave patterns. Stage one is light sleep. We are easily aroused from this stage. Stage two is when we become disconnected from our surroundings and breathing and heart rate are reduced. Stages three and four are deep sleep during which brain restorative functions take place such as brain tissue and cell repair. It is during these stages our brain stores memory of recent events. Stage five is called REM sleep (for rapid-eye-movement sleep). Here again we are in light sleep and do most of our dreaming. On average about 10 percent is stage one, 50 percent stage two, 20 percent stages three and four, and 20 percent stage five, REM sleep. These five stages of sleep repeat themselves throughout the night in roughly 90-minute cycles.

There are physical reasons we do not have the same sleep patterns and abilities we had when we were younger. As we age, many things cause us to wake more often. Bathroom trips and joint and muscle aches and pains lead the list. We tend to have more trouble getting to sleep and returning to sleep after awakening. As we age we have less deep sleep in stages three and four. In fact some seniors have very little or no deep sleep. When our sleep is lighter we tend to wake more frequently. Some general rules can be useful. Like with any advice, we all are individuals and the following are just guides:

- What you do during the day can affect your nighttime sleep. It's common knowledge that caffeine can cause poor sleep. Many seniors limit coffee to the morning hours expecting the effects of caffeine to be minimal by evening. Remember that other liquids like non-herbal teas and many carbonated drinks contain caffeine as does chocolate. (The chocolate cake dessert after dinner may be what keeps you up at night.) Avoid eating a meal for four hours before bedtime—a small snack may be fine. Alcohol may make you drowsy, but the sleep it promotes is not natural. Here again, a small amount may be tolerated well, but anything more should be avoided. Lastly, nicotine is a stimulant and needs to be avoided even in secondhand smoke.
- As a general rule 7–8 hours of sleep a night is sufficient for most seniors. One of the ways to test your needs is to turn off any alarm clock or wake-up call, go to bed at the same time each night for two weeks, and sleep until you wake up naturally in the morning. The average number of hours you slept is an estimate of your sleep needs.
- There are several important points about where you sleep. Most sleep specialists suggest a bedroom should be used for sleep and sex. Television sets, reading, and electronic devices should be enjoyed in another part of your dwelling. If you can't sleep, get up and go to another room and do something until you get tired and feel like going back to sleep.
- The sleeping room should be free of extraneous light and noise, cool enough to use at least one cover, and have a comfortable mattress. You can compensate with eye shades or a terry cloth

towel over your eyes to reduce light and ear plugs for noise distractions.

- Exercising early in the day is good for many reasons. It also exposes you to sunshine, which makes more melatonin, a natural chemical that promotes sleep.
- If you take a nap, doing it earlier in the day helps.
- Wind down for an hour before you go to bed with relaxed reading, gentle music, meditation, or relaxation techniques. Focus on deep breathing: try slowly inhaling to the count of four, holding your breath to the count of two, and slowly exhale to the count of four. Repeat as many times as needed (adapted from the book *Metahuman* by Deepak Chopra).
- Check tomorrow's calendar and make a to-do list, so it doesn't keep you awake at night.
- If nothing seems to work you may need to seek medical advice. Ask your provider if any of your medications may be affecting your sleep. There are several sleep disorders to consider. Sleep apnea—where your throat tissues relax and obstruct your airway during sleep—can cause you to wake up several times an hour. Emotional stress can can keep you awake at night. If severe it may require a consultation with a medical provider. Sleepwalking is rare, but can be dangerous and needs urgent attention.

RESOURCES:

These are some of the things to think about. National organizations have much more information. The following is a reliable resource:

National Sleep Foundation. https://www.thensf.org

FALLING

Falls are one of the most preventable senior health problems. Learning how to prevent falls can make or break a life well lived.

An excellent resource can be found at Centers for Disease Control and Prevention. Their summary of home and recreation safety is a good place to start. The data show that one in four seniors over age sixty-five fall each year. Only half of the falls are reported to their doctor. If you have fallen once, you double your chances of falling again. One out of five falls results in broken bones or head injuries.

In the United States, 3 million older adults are treated in emergency departments for falls each year. Over 25 percent are hospitalized, mostly for head injuries and hip fractures. At least 300,000 older people are hospitalized for hip fractures and at least 95 percent of those are caused from falls, mostly falling sideways. Falls are the most common cause of traumatic brain injury. The total medical cost in 2015 was more than $50 billion. Medicare and Medicaid paid 75 percent of the costs.

Why do we fall so often? The physical changes that come with aging are the major contributing factors. When we get out of bed or up from a chair, our blood pressure makes adjustments. These adjustments slow as we age. We get dizzy or faint when not enough blood flow reaches our brain. Our diminishing visual acuity, which can affect our driving, can also affect our ability to see in our homes—especially at night. Hearing loss makes us less aware of our surroundings, and the inner-ear balance function can make us unsteady. Also our muscle coordination is diminished making automatic body adjustments less effective, which also affects our balance.

Some specific diseases that increase our chances of falling include most of the common disorders. Congestive heart failure, heart-rhythm irregularities, high-blood-pressure treatments, and chronic-lung diseases reduce our ability to get blood flow and oxygen to important tissues, especially to our muscles and brain. Arthritis, skeletal deformity, muscle weakness, chronic pain, and neurological disease are other disorders that make us more susceptible to falls.

Medications are another factor increasing our risk. Blood-pressure drugs, diuretics, antidepressants, sedatives, and tranquilizers are associated with falls. Often there are multiple factors that enter into our susceptibility to fall.

Many of us develop a fear of falling as we get older and less nimble. Researchers have shown that individuals who fear falling become less active. Being less active leads to more muscle weakness, which increases our chance of falling—a vicious cycle of inactivity and decreased muscle strength. To overcome this cycle, regular and safe physical activity can improve our muscle strength no matter how old and frail we are.

What can we do to prevent falling? First, we should talk with our doctor or healthcare provider about our risk of falling. Ask if we should be taking vitamin D supplements for bone health. Ask the pharmacist to review our medications to see if any of them might make us dizzy or sleepy. Ask for alternatives, if one or more of our medications can adversely affect us. Be sure to mention any over-the-counter medications.

Muscle strengthening and balance exercises will help. Many health plans, fitness centers and other organizations offer fitness classes for seniors including Tai Chi, yoga, and Pilates. Tai Chi has been shown to be particularly effective in improving balance in older individuals. Most seniors do not get enough exercise—both endurance and strength. Becoming more physically active is critically important in fall prevention.

Have a vision check each year, especially if using bifocal glasses that can create problems judging distances. Get rid of small area rugs and any uneven surfaces in our homes. Make sure we have lots of lighting with bright bulbs in our home and night-lights in our bed and bathrooms.

There are some specific assistive devices that every senior needs—

grab bars at appropriate locations in our bathrooms and double railings on stairways. We should not be afraid to use a walking stick, cane, or a walker. More sophisticated equipment like wheelchairs, electric chairs, and scooters can offer mobility when needed.

CONSIDERATIONS:

- *Talk with your doctor or care provider about your risk of falling.*

- *Talk with your pharmacist about your medications.*

- *Start or continue strength and balance exercises.*

- *Have a yearly vision check.*

- *Have a periodic hearing check.*

- *Evaluate your floor surfaces.*

- *Check your home lighting.*

- *Be sure the grab bars in your bathroom are located where you need them.*

- *Use assistive devices (walking stick, cane, walker, etc.) when unsteady.*

RESOURCES:

Centers for Disease Control and Prevention, National Center for Injury Prevention and Control. Web-based Injury Statistics Query and Reporting System (WISOARS): https://www.cdc.gov>falls

Hackney, M. E., Wolf, S. L., Fahd, F. "Tai Chu'an Practice on Balance and Mobility in Older Adults: An Integrative Review of 20 years of Research." *Geriatric Physical Therapy*: July/September 2014: Vol 37, pp. 137–135.

KEEPING WELL IN MIND AND BODY

Our brain controls our lives. It is the center of wakefulness and the subconscious that affects everything we do. The billions of nerve cells and the trillions of neurological connections are continually being modified. Some are lost, but we are learning that new connections can be made throughout life. The old theory of irreversibly losing brain cells as we age has been disproven.

The brain cells and their chemical transmitters process information that controls and influences body activity such as movement, sensation, wakefulness, sleep, appetite, and the emotions of fear, pleasure, and excitement. Millions of neurochemical programs are functioning continuously. These functions can be stimulated externally by our senses. Or they can be stimulated by internal signals such as hunger, pain, thought, and memory.

New learning adds to our brain's growing database throughout our lives. Unfortunately, there are conditions and events that can interrupt healthy growth and function. Head injury, even minor trauma, can damage brain function temporarily or permanently. The skull becomes a solid boney structure after early childhood to protect the intricate and delicate structures and functions inside. We need to take any head injury seriously. Even a slight bump on the head can cause bleeding from small blood vessels inside the skull.

The second major brain disorder we risk as we age is the deranged repair of brain cells causing tangles and/or abnormal deposits of foreign proteins. These processes disrupt the brain cells' normal function and manifest as memory loss such as Alzheimer's disease, or abnormal physical activity such as Parkinsonism. Scientists have worked hard trying to understand the human brain—how it develops, maintains itself, and how it loses function. Our brain is what makes us human. But we don't have full knowledge of our brain and our treatments of known brain disorders are still in the early stages of development.

Scientists have recently reported that physical muscular exercise can actually stimulate nerve connections. We know that mental activity, particularly new learning, stimulates functional brain growth. And now we have another reason to exercise regularly as we learn about the positive effect of muscular exercise. A good diet, plenty of water, adequate sleep, no smoking, alcohol in moderation, and regular physical exercise are needed to maintain our brain's health and to even increase its capabilities. It is important to move beyond our routines and try to deal with the unfamiliar by taking up mentally, physically, and socially challenging activities. We are learning that our brains grow more fit when we learn new things.

Advice on the following five areas can improve our mental well-being.

MOOD

There is a strong correlation between optimism and health. How can we create a positive attitude and a positive mood?

- Smiling a lot helps.
- Choosing to be positive makes a difference. Even if we feel indifferent or blue, choosing to be optimistic and positive will make us and those around us feel better and enjoy life more.
- Laughing releases brain endorphins that make us feel good.
- Saying thank you often and being grateful.
- Seeking pleasant environments such as going on a nature walk, listening to pleasing music, wearing bright colors, or recalling a pleasant memory.
- Reaching out to others, accepting invitations, attending a concert, a play, or an art exhibition.
- Listing or saying what you can do well.

FOCUS

- Do tasks during the best times of our day.
- Consciously think "I'm going to focus."
- Avoid multitasking because it detracts from focusing.
- Avoid external distractions.
- Maintain focus, and consciously refocus when distracted.
- Feed our brains with new activities.
- Reduce stress by planning ahead, allocating enough time, performing breathing exercises, meditating, or doing what we have found that works.
- Create a goal and reward yourself for progress.
- Take a break and do something else for a while.
- Jot down random thoughts for later use and return to your focused activity.
- Try using your opposite hand for writing, brushing teeth, and dialing the phone.
- Wear your watch upside down for a day or two.

WORDS AND MEMORY

Reading, writing, speaking, and listening all use different parts of our brain. We begin to lose some of our word and name recall about the age of forty. It can be noticeable and distressing even though we know it is common. With each decade the process can become more troublesome, but there are strategies that can help us as we age.

- Associate a new word or name with other similar words, the same beginning sound, the same number of syllables, the same stress pattern, or a rhyming word.
- Try searching down the alphabet for the beginning letter of the word or name.
- Focus on words that come to mind while searching. It may restore the connection.
- Make a mental connection between the new word and something you know such as Florence, Italy, for the name Florence.
- Repeat the word several times. Say it out loud if appropriate or write it down. Each method uses a different part of our brain.
- Use the word emotionally or sing it.

- Motivate yourself by saying, "I'm going to remember this word/name."
- Try some word or number games. Scrabble is one. Card games like bridge, cribbage, canasta, and rummy challenge the brain.
- See how many words you can write for each letter in the alphabet in two minutes.
- Choose a long word like "innovation" and see how many words you can make using only those letters.
- Say or write all the words you can from a particular category (such as animals, trees, countries, colors, US states, etc.).

STRESS and BREATHING

Stressing one's physical actions and mental activity can be enjoyable and productive. But when healthy stress turns into distress, the body and mind begin to break down. Relaxation strategies such as meditation, mindfulness, visualization, yoga, Tai Chi, and breathing exercises all focus on the moment and use purposeful nonjudgmental acceptance of one's thoughts and feelings. They promote calmness, compassion, learning, memory, and decrease brain stress. Some strategies to reduce stress include:

- Diaphragmatic breathing promotes calming through the parasympathetic nervous system.

  Lie down or sit comfortably in a chair with one hand on your chest and the other hand on your abdomen just below your ribcage. Relax. Inhale deeply through your nose, expanding your abdomen while trying not to expand your chest—this is called abdominal breathing. Slowly exhale through tightened (pursed) lips using your abdominal and not your chest muscles. Practice using just your abdominal muscles.

- Relaxation techniques are usually practiced away from distractions and focus on one thing.

  1. Meditation has various forms (transcendental, focused breathing, repetitive word or phrase, or visual image). Let thoughts fade away and focus on your word or image with each breath. (Expect to spend 20–30 minutes for each session. Professional training is useful.)

2. Mindfulness is a form of meditation that emphasizes an awareness of immediate sensations and surroundings. Overall well-being is enhanced by mind and body being in the same place.

3. Visualize a brief journey to a favorite place, thing, or image. Imagine the journey in your mind and then retrace the journey back to where you started. (This can be a form of self-hypnosis.)

   Example: Sarah had trouble sleeping during her husband's protracted illness. She would visualize sitting on precambrian rock on the North Shore of Lake Superior and imagine acupuncture points while drifting off to sleep.

4. Left and right nasal breathing: use your thumb and fourth finger to alternately close your nostrils. Depress your right nostril and slowly inhale and exhale, then close your left nostril and slowly inhale and exhale. Repeat each sequence 10 times.

5. Progressive relaxation: breathe into and exhale to relax each part of your body, starting with your toes and progressing to your head. A similar progression can be done by tightening and relaxing your muscles from your toes to your head.

   Example: Ray was a student who had a bedtime ritual. When he was settled for sleep and closed his eyes, he slowly said, "Good night toes, good night feet, good night knees, etc." By the time he reached his hips he had usually drifted off to sleep.

- Breathing routines:

  1. Simply observe your breathing 2–3 times a day on a regular basis.
  2. Habitually take one deep mindful breath at specific times of the day.
  3. Sit in a comfortable upright position with eyes closed. Notice your body and the movement of your breathing.

CREATIVITY

We discussed how to find meaning and purposeful living in chapter 2. Participate in a writer's group. Take up an artistic activity such as dance, music, or drama, or make art, painting, poetry, flower arranging, sculpture, or collage. These new things stimulate our brains, create new connections, and generate reserve brain capacity. If we are active and thoughtful, we reduce our chances of developing significant memory deficits as we age. The human brain is a remarkable organ. Take good care of it.

feeling blue

FEELING BLUE

Most of us would like to feel great all the time, but life doesn't work that way. We all have periods where we feel down, listless, or unusually tired. We can literally feel depressed. Then there are times we get emotionally upset and can't seem to settle down. We get anxious and unsettled at the smallest stress. If these feelings persist for days or weeks, the feelings are called depression and anxiety.

How do we know when we are in need of help? We might be reluctant to share our negative feelings with others, but we can begin by talking to a family member or a friend. Emotional or intellectual barriers should not keep us from seeing a professional. Talk therapy and/or medications can be effective. Some find it helpful to write down their feelings and their concerns and then return to these at a later time. The following self-rated depression scale for seniors was developed by Sheikh and Yesavage to help us identify the difference from the ups and downs of normal living and the clinical depressions that might benefit from seeking professional help.

Circle the best answer for how you felt over the last week.

1. Are you basically satisfied with your life? YES / *NO*

2. Have you dropped many of your activities and interests? *YES* / NO

3. Do you feel your life is empty? *YES* / NO

4. Do you often get bored? *YES* / NO

5. Are you in good spirits most of the time? YES / *NO*

6. Are you afraid something bad is going to happen to you? *YES* / NO

7. Do you feel happy most of the time? YES / *NO*

8. Do you often feel helpless? *YES* / NO

9. Do you prefer to stay at home, rather than going out and doing new things? *YES* / NO

10. Do you feel you have more problems with memory than most people? *YES* / NO

11. Do you think it is wonderful to be alive? YES / *NO*

12. Do you feel pretty worthless the way you are now? *YES* / NO

13. Do you feel full of energy? YES / *NO*

14. Do you feel that your situation is hopeless? *YES* / NO

15. Do you think that most people are better off than you are? *YES* / NO

Answers indicating depression are in bold and italicized. Score one point for each bold answer circled. A score of 0 to 5 suggests normal. A score higher than 5 suggests depression.

Turning to anxiety, how do we know if the tension and the nervousness we feel is abnormal and would benefit from some type of intervention? It is normal to feel stressed at times, such as when starting something new, having to lead a group, or taking a trip. Mental Health America is a non-profit organization that has developed a set of screening questions to help us learn if our anxieties would benefit from a professional consultation.

ANXIETY SCREENING TEST

Over the last two weeks, how often have you been bothered by the following problems?

	Not at all	Several days	More than half the days	Nearly every day
1. Feeling nervous, anxious, or on edge?				
2. Not being able to stop or control worrying?				
3. Worrying too much about different things?				
4. Having trouble relaxing?				
5. Feeling afraid that something awful might happen?				

Neither of these screening tools are diagnostic, but they can be useful to you and your medical providers. Some of the questions might help you understand why you feel the way you do and whether you might benefit from discussing your feelings with your physician or medical-care provider.

RESOURCES:

Sheikh, J.I., Yesavage, J.A. "Geriatric Depression Scale (GDS): Recent Evidence and Development of a Shorter Version." *Clinical Gerontologist.* June, 1986, pp. 165–173.

Primary Care Evaluation of Mental Health Disorders Patient Health Questionnaire (PRIME-MD-PHQ) developed by Drs. Robert L. Spritzer, Janet B.W. Williams, Kurt Knoenke and colleagues. https://www.mhanational.org/programs.

RECOGNIZING FRAUD

Unwanted communication is one of the downsides of our telephone, internet, and modern mail systems. We love the access to relatives and friends and the access to the world of information. But with the benefits comes a downside. No matter how we struggle, we are interrupted with unwanted calls and the risk of being defrauded. How we deal with the current cyberworld can be detrimental to our physical, mental, and financial health.

First, what to do about robocalls? No matter how our governments have tried, the calls keep coming. The do-not-call list has not reduced unwanted calls. Not all robocalls are scams, but they are annoying. Telemarketing is a big business. One way to reduce their frequency is to never make a monetary commitment over the phone. Ask for a mail solicitation, if you are interested in the product or organization. Another method is not to answer unrecognized numbers or hang up if you recognize the caller is soliciting money or unwanted products.

How do we avoid scams where fraudsters attempt to intimidate us into transferring money to them? Here are some guidelines that might help reduce your risk of being defrauded.

1. Never say "yes" when the caller asks, "Are you _____ (and gives your name)." They might be recording your voice to use in authorizing a financial transaction. Simply ask, "Who is

calling" without giving your name. If you don't recognize the caller, hang up before getting into a discussion.

2. If you have caller ID, the number may look like it is coming from your area or even your phone exchange. Don't be fooled. It may be a caller from any part of the world who is using a local number.

3. Never give a credit-card number, social security number, bank-account number, or any financial information to any unsolicited caller, even if they claim to represent a company you know. Be sure you are dealing with a trusted person and a legitimate organization, even if you initiate the contacts. Many scams over the telephone or internet start with a free offer that looks very attractive. The item may be free, but there is a mailing or handling fee that requires a credit-card payment. Never give your credit-card number to obtain a free gift. The offer may be legitimate, but don't take a chance.

4. Charities continue to make unsolicited fund-raising calls. They request you give or make a pledge over the phone. Don't do it. Ask them to send their literature in the mail so you can consider their request at your leisure. One technique is to take all the requests and make your charitable decisions at a certain time once a year, perhaps in November or December. You may have many requests from the same organization that is trying to get you to make multiple contributions and expecting you to forget when or how often they have received your support. Giving to charity is important, but don't be led to contribute more than you intend.

5. The IRS never contacts taxpayers by telephone, email, texts, or social media to request personal or financial information. Any call that threatens lawsuits or arrests are never from the IRS.

6. As a general rule, hang up on any robocall, ignore any claims, and avoid schemes that involve sending money orders, prepaid cards, or gift cards to anyone you don't know. Legitimate companies rarely ask for payment this way.

7. Ignore anyone claiming on the phone to being a government official. Social Security, Medicare, Medicaid, and other government agencies make their notices in writing, not over the phone or internet.

8. If a company tells you over the phone, by email, or by text that your computer has a virus or needs to be protected, don't respond. Take your computer to a trusted repair shop to check for viruses.

9. If you get a call that a friend or loved one needs emergency money, call the loved one directly and determine the need.

10. Before sending any money, you can check out the company and the offer with the State Attorney General and the Better Business Bureau.

The telephone isn't the only method used by fraudsters. Emails and texts are another way they get into our lives. The same actions listed above should be applied to any questionable inquiry. Be suspicious of any unfamiliar contact. Even what looks like a known sender can be fake. Spot a phishing email by verifying the sender's email address. Scammers will misspell, change numbers, add characters, etc., to make it look like a legitimate email address or domain name. Most legitimate companies and organizations have anti-fraud processes in place, but you can't rely solely on them to eliminate your risk. Seniors are at particularly high risk. We are deemed to be easier targets and therefore are more likely to be subjected to phishing, scams, and other fraudulent activity. Remain on guard. Be suspicious of any unsolicited communication. Some of the common scams have earned their own names—The Grandparent/Grandchild scam; Fake Check scam; Medicare scams; Tech-Support scams; Investment scams; Work-at-Home scams; Lottery scams; Personal and Medical Safety Product scams; "You Have Won" scams; Bogus Charity scams; Living Trust scams. Err on the side of caution and don't let someone take advantage of you.

Anyone using credit of any kind should review their credit report at least once a year or when you detect any suspicious activity. Freezing your credit is one way to protect yourself from an unauthorized person opening an account in your name. You can freeze and unfreeze your credit by contacting each of the credit agencies.

Periodic credit reports from the three major companies are free. They may try to sell you one of their services, but you don't have to buy anything to get a full report. The three major credit reporting agencies are: Experian: 1-888-397-3742; TransUnion: 1-800-916-8800; and Equifax: 1-800-685-1111. They all can also be contacted online.

RESOURCES:

State Attorney General's Office

Local Better Business Bureau

Senior Organizations

Federal Trade Commission
    Bureau of Consumer Protection
    600 Pennsylvania Avenue NW
    Washington, DC 20580
    (877) 382-4357
    www.consumer.ftc.gov

PART TWO

Healthcare Issues

OUR AGING BODIES

Why do we achieve our maximum physical and mental capabilities as we grow and develop into adulthood and then begin to decline? Athletes peak in their twenties and thirties and then their physical capacities decline. Physicists do their most creative work early in their careers, but artists and writers can create great work as they age. Wisdom comes from experiences just as our physical capabilities are beginning to decline. What actually is happening as we physically age?

Animal bodies are complex functioning organisms. Humans have the most complex brains of all the animals as far as we know. Many species physically outperform us in speed, agility, strength, but our mental abilities surpass all others. Billions of neurochemical programs are continuously functioning to keep the cells in our organs functioning. These reactions require constant maintenance and replacement throughout our lives. There is much we don't know about aging, but we do know that some of our body's maintenance and repair functions slow as we age. We build up immunity to infections we encounter throughout our lives. But this immunity wanes as we age. During normal development the tendency of our cells to grow indefinitely is kept in balance and prevents cancer as growth, repair, and maintenance take place early in life. As we age, our body's ability to repair weak cells and control the growth of cells is diminished. Loss of brain connections, high-frequency hearing loss, reduced vision, weaker muscles, deteriorating joints, reduced heart function, trouble controlling blood sugar, and the growth of malignancies become more frequent.

Our understanding of the aging process progresses year by year. We have discussed some of the preventive actions seniors can take in earlier chapters. While we can't eliminate the physical and mental changes of aging, there are actions we can take that can reduce the effects and make our lives better.

Many of us enjoy alcoholic beverages. However, we are less able to tolerate the effects of alcohol as we age. The one to two drink adult recommendations need to be modified. Being aware that we are less able to safely consume what was well tolerated in the past is important to keep in mind.

Our reduced mobility, slower reaction time, muscular weakness, and bone fragility contribute to our instability and make us more vulnerable to injuring ourselves (or others when we are driving). Visual and hearing losses make our everyday living more challenging in spite of eye glasses and hearing aids.

Chronic diseases gradually catch up with most of us. It is critical to treat high blood pressure. Heart and other vascular disorders are common and can limit our activity. Diabetes and chronic lung disease may require lifelong medical attention. Arthritis is a given. We all have some, somewhere. If we have had cancer, it can become another chronic disease for us. Our enjoyment of life and even our longevity can depend on how we approach these and other chronic conditions. We need to accept our frailties and the limits on our lives as we age and think about our life ending.

THE END OF LIFE

Most of us look forward to the days, weeks, and years ahead and avoid thinking about the end of our physical lives. Take the time and effort to make some important decisions for you and your loved ones while your mind is clear and you can express your wishes and desires. These next chapters will give you some background for when you might have to make some difficult decisions.

Learn from the experience of others at the end of life. We can overcome our reluctance and inertia when we learn about the successful and less successful experiences of others. Atul Gawande has written a book called *Being Mortal: Medicine and What Matters in the End.* It describes his family's experiences as his surgeon father dealt with a terminal illness. It is a sensitive, yet a frank and reflective discussion of the medical decisions they had to make and the emotions they experienced during the course of his illness. The book is highly recommended as excellent background reading for how we wish to be treated by our family and caregivers as we deal with serious illnesses.

"Being Mortal" is a PBS documentary that follows several patients in their last year of life. The documentary shows live patients interacting with medical consultants and their families as they deal with serious medical problems. It is presented with caring and compassionate interviews with patients, their families, their caregivers, and Dr. Gawande. The video is well worth the fifty minutes it takes to watch it. You can find it online at pbs.org. Click on search and type in "Being Mortal." Choose the *Being Mortal* documentary.

The following six chapters will deal with most of the issues we will face as we approach the end of our lives. We are all writing our own stories, and this section of our guide will end with some real-life examples.

OUR HEALTHCARE SYSTEM

Seniors have more interaction with healthcare professionals and the systems in which they work. Their advice and recommended treatments can provide comfort, relieve symptoms, and save lives. On the other hand, some surgeries, medications, and even diagnostic tests can be painful, time consuming, and meaningless to our long-range health. We will examine these concerns and emphasize the need for seniors to think about the capabilities and the limitations of our current healthcare systems as we approach the end of life.

The first thing to consider is disease prevention. The foundations of good health are: clean water, clean air, nutritious food, personal hygiene, and exercise. Our lifestyle is a major contributor to our well-being. Our chances for good health and long life are reduced if we are obese, if we smoke or vape, if we have unprotected sex, if we are physically inactive, or if we overuse alcohol or other mood-altering substances (e.g., marijuana, methamphetamines, or other street drugs).

We all need a primary-care professional who has agreed to be our medical contact. We need a physician, physician assistant, or nurse practitioner whom we can trust and easily contact when we have an illness or a medical question. Seniors on Medicare are encouraged to see their primary-care contact every year for a review of their health situation. For the amount of time and dollars spent this may be our most valuable medical service. I say, "Just do it."

The healthcare system can help us when we have a problem. The first line of contact in a non-emergency situation is your primary-care provider. If the situation is urgent and you cannot get a timely primary-care appointment, go to a nearby urgent-care center where minor problems can be treated. The third option, if the situation is an emergency or life-threatening, is to go to the emergency department at the nearest hospital.

At any one of these access points of care you will be met with a health professional. Nurses and doctors will assess the situation and begin testing and treatment or refer you to the next level of care, depending on your presumptive diagnosis or diagnoses. You can expect blood tests, urine tests, electrocardiograms, and imaging (X-ray, MRI, CT, and ultrasound). Medications, intravenous fluids, or antibiotics may be prescribed, continued, or changed. Hospitalization may be recommended depending on the severity of your condition and the risk to you or others of continuing treatment at home. Surgical interventions may be recommended for diagnostic biopsy or therapeutic treatment.

Chronic conditions can largely be managed outside of the hospital. Conditions such as diabetes, hypertension, heart disease, arthritis, and cancer can be managed in a medical office or virtual setting. Radiation therapy and chemotherapy are two common interventions for cancer and other conditions that are given inside and outside a hospital.

Life-threatening conditions may require intensive care and life support available in most hospitals. Each level of intensity brings its own complications, discomforts, and expense. Current technology can substitute for most organ functions temporarily, and consciousness can be temporarily suppressed with narcotics and sedatives. Intensive care keeps people alive until their body heals with supplemental oxygen, breathing tubes, mechanical ventilators, cardiac-assist devices, pacemakers, defibrillators, intravenous fluids, feeding tubes, artificial kidney dialysis, bladder catheters, and brain catheters to relieve swelling.

After hospitalization an individual may need rehabilitation. Transitional care for a period of weeks may be recommended before an individual can care for themselves at home. Some individuals may eventually need more permanent placement in a long-term care facility such as a nursing home.

We expect a lot from our healthcare system. Fortunately, almost all senior citizens in the United States have financial access to the whole spectrum of care through Medicare and Medicaid. But there are limitations on what the system can do and how much curative care we are willing to accept. And there are many people living in the United States who are citizens of other countries who do not have access to our government-sponsored programs.

All of us will eventually contract a terminal illness. It may present suddenly, such as a heart attack, or develop slowly as in diabetes and many cancers. If we are capable, we will need to decide how much curative care, as opposed to how much pain relief and comfort-based, quality-of-life care we desire. However, when the time comes, not all of us will be able to make our own decisions. Our designated healthcare agent, our family, or friends will need to make those decisions for us. The more specifically we express our wishes while we are able, the more likely our decisions will be respected when we are unable to make our wishes known.

Complications from medical and surgical interventions are not rare in elderly patients. Broken ribs from cardiopulmonary resuscitation (CPR) are common. Chemotherapy and radiation can make people feel sick. Pain and sedation medications can make patients drowsy or incoherent when they want to be awake to talk to their loved ones. Medications that we needed and tolerated when we were stable can now lead to undesirable side effects as our bodies get weaker. At some point any further medical intervention becomes futile. At that point the benefit of further curative treatment becomes negligible and our suffering will be prolonged.

Patients maintain autonomy. You can decide if you want specific medical care. You have a right to accept or refuse any care or treatments at any time. Continuing intensive treatments, limiting some interventions, or withdrawing all life-sustaining measures are made by you, the patient. If you are unable to express your wishes, your healthcare agent will use your advance directive, if you have one. Caregivers will voice their assessments and advice, but insurance companies and hospital administrators have to stand back as the decisions are made by you or your designated representatives. Families who have discussed these issues beforehand and are aware of the patient's wishes, preferably in a written advanced directive, are better equipped to make the hard decisions when they come up. Having an advanced directive, sometimes called a living will, is an important document for these critical discussions.

Patient comfort is always part of any medical treatment. When decisions authorize caregivers to focus on relief of pain and suffering at the end of life, they are skilled at providing pain medications and sedation. Palliative-care consultations are frequently held at any time during serious illness. Hospice care is recognized as an important capability in the last six months of life, and it is usually funded by Medicare and Medicaid. Hospice services associated with a hospital have a high level of accountability and may be the best choice when available. When end-of-life wishes have been discussed by the patient with their family and healthcare agents, preferably written in an advance directive, there rarely is a conflict that requires a hospital ethics committee, lawyers, or a judge to get involved.

Medical-aid-in-dying is a term used for a patient who legally takes a self-administered lethal dose of prescribed medications. Many of our states allow two physicians to certify that a dying patient is in their last six months of expected life, is not depressed, and is competent to make the decision to end their own life. In those states physicians can write an order for lethal oral medications for patients to take at a time of their choosing. Many other states are considering legislation to make this option legal. Anyone considering medical-aid-in-dying, beyond the support of hospice care, should contact their primary medical team or legal sources in their state.

HOSPICE AND PALLIATIVE CARE

Hospice care and palliative care are two medical terms about care to manage the chronic discomfort from conditions that are not likely to be cured. While these medical services have some overlap, they differ in scope and timing.

Palliative care is a comprehensive approach provided by care teams to improve the quality of life for individuals who are living with serious illnesses. Palliative-care services work to relieve pain and discomfort. The services work with the patient, the patient's family, and the primary-care team not only to relieve discomfort, but to support the physical, emotional, and spiritual needs of the patient and family. A team of specially trained physicians, nurses, therapists, social workers, counselors, therapists, and aides bring their expertise to address the specific needs and desires of an individual patient and family. Every patient is different, and a palliative team will make recommendations and will design a care plan to meet the patient's needs. Most palliative-care consultations and services will be covered by Medicare and other insurance providers.

Palliative care can be helpful for patients with congestive heart failure, chronic obstructive lung disease (COPD), cancer, kidney failure, Parkinson's disease, liver failure, Alzheimer's disease, and other dementias. The philosophy of palliative care is to relieve symptoms and improve one's quality of life when the underlying conditions can't be cured. Pain control and other comfort measures are the first priority. Palliative care reduces stress and discomfort for the patient and family members. Some patients choose to continue treatments such as chemotherapy, radiation, and medications to slow their disease. Others may decide to stop treatments that make them feel worse and choose only pain relief, comfort, and supportive care.

Palliative care can be provided in an outpatient clinic, in a hospital, or in a patient's home. It's important to know that it can be initiated months and years before one is near the end of life. And there is no time limit.

Hospice care is reserved for those patients who are nearing the end of life and are ready to forgo further attempts at curative treatments. Medicare pays for most of the services, but there are several requirements. First, does the Medicare-insured patient have a terminal illness that is expected to last six months or less? The six-month rule is not hard and fast and can be extended, if the patient lives longer than expected. Also hospice services can be cancelled at any time. A medical provider certifies the individual has a terminal illness and is in the last six months of life expectancy. A medical-provider visit is required at least every three months. Again the focus is on improving the patient's quality of life, making the patient comfortable, and maintaining dignity. Usually all curative treatments are stopped, but there is some flexibility. Care may be delivered in the patient's home, a nursing home, a dedicated hospice-care facility, or, rarely, in a hospital.

Patients entering hospice care choose to stop attempts to cure their underlying disease. They may continue medications to manage conditions like blood pressure, heart conditions, diabetes, etc. Each patient is different, and it is up to the patient as to what makes them most comfortable and stable. There is no requirement to remain in hospice. A patient can decide to restart curative treatments at any time or leave hospice if their condition improves.

It is comforting to know that during our last weeks and months of living that we and our family will have the care we need. We can be in control, and our last days will not consume what's left of our finances or put our family in debt.

An example: Fern (not her real name) began having intractable pain down her leg following her third back surgery in her late eighties. Surgeons could not offer further surgical intervention due to her severe arthritis and the scarring of her spine. Over a period of weeks, pain medications were adjusted to the point where she was comfortable and could do most of the things she wanted to do. She was taught how to apply narcotic skin patches every three days and how to use supplementary oral pain medications when needed. For nearly a decade she was able to manage this palliative treatment with the aid of her primary physician.

In Fern's ninety-eighth year she had a stroke that required her to live in a skilled-nursing facility. About six months later she developed a persistent ulcer on one of her little toes. The circulation to her foot was compromised. An angiogram showed almost no arterial blood flow beyond her knee. There was no hope of repairing or bypassing the severely diseased arteries. The vascular surgeon gave her two choices: above-the-knee amputation or pain control and hospice. She refused an amputation.

Over the next few days her pain medications were adjusted, and she was admitted to hospice care while continuing her current living arrangement. Over the next several months she was comfortable and was able to have many conversations with her family, friends, and caregivers. As she became weaker, her family gathered at her bedside for her final hours. One of the family members said, " She taught us so many things in her 99 years, and now she has taught us how to die."

Health Care Planning

END-OF-LIFE PLANNING

There are two major things to consider when thinking about your physical life coming to a close—how you want to be treated by those around you and how to assure that your wishes are carried out if you are not able to communicate with your caregivers. These decisions should be written down and shared with those close to you.

There are formal methods of communicating your end-of-life wishes. Living Wills are now more appropriately call Healthcare Directives. A healthcare directive gives you an opportunity to document how you wish to be treated by healthcare professionals when you have serious medical problems. For instance, you can specify whether or not you want breathing support, if you can't breathe, or your heart restarted, if it stops. You can state that you want all intensive care available unless there is no reasonable hope of recovery. If there is no hope of recovery, you can state that you wish to be kept comfortable until the end. Or you can be more specific, "I want antibiotics and other medications but no breathing machines and no cardiac resuscitation." Most people discuss their options and choices with their physicians and family members, but each individual ultimately makes their own choices. Do you want extensive medical interventions or a certain quality of life for the time remaining? All contingencies can't be anticipated in advance, but the more specific you can be, the more likely you will receive the care you desire.

An integral part of your healthcare directive is the selection of a Healthcare Agent. This is a trusted person who knows your wishes and has agreed to act in your behalf when you cannot make healthcare decisions yourself. Selecting your agent is important. It should be a person you trust—a spouse, a family member, a close friend, a lawyer, or your clergy. Generic healthcare directive forms are included with this guide (see an example at the end of this chapter). It must be signed by you and witnessed by a notary or two other persons.

A completed Healthcare Directive should identify you, your address, phone numbers, and where copies of your directive have been sent or are located.

Part 1 names your healthcare agent and her/his relationship and contact information. It is wise to also name an alternative agent just in case. Neither your primary nor alternate agent can be a medical provider who might be caring for you unless they are legally related to you by marriage, adoption, etc. Your agent will make choices about your medical care based on the instructions in your healthcare directive. You can state specific limits on their authority if you wish.

Part 2 is optional and gives you an opportunity to express your thoughts and feelings: what makes your life worth living; your beliefs about when life is no longer worth living; choices of specific medical treatments you want or don't want; and thoughts about where you would like to spend your last days and hours. There is space to note your religious affiliation, organ-donation wishes, and any specific rituals, prayers, music, etc., you would like.

Part 3 gives you the opportunity to describe what life-prolonging treatments you desire and what you do not desire. It specifically asks about cardiopulmonary resuscitation (CPR) if your heart stops or you can't breathe.

Part 4 is where your witnessed signature makes this a legal document.

Once your healthcare directive is completed and signed, copies should be made for your healthcare agent, your primary physician (physician's assistant, or nurse practitioner), your lawyer, your family members, and for your files. It's a good idea to post it in a prominent place, such as your refrigerator door, if you do not want life-sustaining treatment in an emergency.

Along with the paper document, we recommend you start oral conversations with your healthcare agent and your family to explain your reasoning and to seek their understanding if not their agreement. This notifies people in your life of your current wishes. You can change or revise your healthcare directive at any time. It is a good practice to review it once a year, and to review it with your healthcare agent, especially when there is a significant change in your physical condition or a change in your social environment.

Minnesota Health Care Directive

This document replaces any health care directive made before this one.

This document doesn't apply to electroconvulsive therapy or neuroleptic medications for mental illness.

I will give copies to my health care agents and health care teams when completed.

I will make a new health care directive if my agents, goals, preferences, or instructions change.

My Full Name _____ **My Date of Birth** _____

My Address _____

My Cell # _____ **Home #** _____ **Work #** _____

My Health Care Agents

My health care agent is my voice if I can't make health care decisions for myself. I trust my agent to **be my advocate,** to **follow my instructions,** and to **make decisions based on what I would want**. My agents are at least 18 years old. If I chose my health care provider to be an agent, I have given my reason below.

Health Care Agent

Name_____Relationship to me_____

Address_____

Cell #_____ Home #_____ Work #_____

First Alternate Health Care Agent-If my health care agent isn't willing, able, or reasonably available.

Name_____Relationship to me_____

Address_____

Cell #_____ Home #_____ Work #_____

Second Alternate Health Care Agent-If my first alternate agent isn't willing, able, or reasonably available.

Name_____Relationship to me_____

Address_____

Cell #_____ Home #_____ Work #_____

Why I chose these health care agents: _____

_____

Health Care Agents: Powers and Special Situations

If I'm not able to make my own health care decisions, my health care agent can: access my medical records, decide when to start and stop treatments, and choose my health care team and place of care.

I also want my health care agent to:

☐ Make decisions about continuing a pregnancy if I can't make them myself.

☐ Make decisions about the care of my body after death (autopsy, burial, cremation).

Name_____ Date_____

My Goals and Values

These answers should be used to help make health care decisions if I can't make them myself.

Three non-medical things I want others to know about me:

What gives me strength or keeps me going in difficult times:

My worries and fears about my health:

My goals if my health gets worse:

What I want others to know about my spiritual, cultural, religious, or other beliefs:

Things that make my life worth living:

When I am nearing death, I would find comfort and support from:

My idea of a good death is:

Name_____ Date_____

Life-Sustaining Treatments

Mechanical or artificial treatments may keep a person alive when the body can't function on its own. Examples are: ventilation (breathing machine) when the lungs aren't working, cardiopulmonary resuscitation (CPR) to try to restart a heart that has stopped beating, artificial feeding through tubes, intravenous (IV) fluids, and dialysis when the kidneys aren't working.

My Future Care Preferences if I'm Permanently Unconscious

Permanent unconsciousness can be caused by an accident, a stroke, and other illnesses. My health care team may call this a **permanent vegetative state.** This means the brain is so badly hurt that the person isn't aware of self or others, can't understand or communicate, and the health care team believes the person won't get better.

If I'm permanently unconscious:

☐ **I want some or all possible life-sustaining treatments** if I'm permanently unconscious.
My health care agent should work with my health care team to make decisions about treatments based on my goals and values.

OR

☐ **I don't want life-sustaining treatments** if I'm permanently unconscious.
Focus on making me comfortable and allow natural death.

OR

☐ **I can't make a decision now about life-sustaining treatments** if I'm permanently unconscious.
My health care agent should work with my health care team to decide whether or not to use life-sustaining treatments based on my goals and values.

My Future Care Preferences if I'm Terminally Ill

A terminal condition means **no cure is possible** and **death is expected in the near future**. This can be caused by: failure of vital organs (including end-stage heart failure, lung failure, kidney failure, and liver failure), advanced cancer, advanced dementia, a massive heart attack or stroke, and other causes.

If I'm terminally ill:

☐ **I want some or all possible life-sustaining treatments** if I'm terminally ill.
My health care agent should work with my health care team to make decisions about treatments based on my goals and values.

OR

☐ **I don't want life-sustaining treatments** if I'm terminally ill.
Focus on making me comfortable and allow natural death.

OR

☐ **I can't make a decision now about life-sustaining treatments** if I'm terminally ill.
My health care agent should work with my health care team to decide whether or not to use life-sustaining treatments based on my goals and values.

Name_____ Date_____

Organ Donation

☐ **I want to donate my eyes, tissues and/or organs, if I can.** My health care agent may start and continue any treatments needed until the donation is complete.

☐ **I don't want to donate my eyes, tissues and/or organs.**

After I Die

These are my wishes about **what to do with my body after I have died** (autopsy, burial, cremation, etc.) and **how I wish to be remembered** (obituary, funeral, memorial service, etc.):

Additional Instructions

☐ I have attached #_____ page(s) of additional instructions to this document.

Making This Document Legal

1. **Sign and date:** *My Signature* _____ *Date Signed* _____

2. **Have your signature notarized OR verified by 2 witnesses**

   MINNESOTA NOTARY PUBLIC: County of _____(county name)   NOTARY SEAL
   In my presence on the date of _____(date notarized)   BELOW
   _____ (person signing above)
   acknowledged their signature on this document. I am not named as a health care
   agent in this document.
   Signature of Notary _____

   OR

   STATEMENT OF WITNESSES: I am at least 18 years old. I am not named as a health care agent in this document. Only one witness can be an employee of the health care system providing care to the person on this date.

   Witness # 1 Signature _____ *Witness # 2 Signature* _____

   Date Signed _____ *Date Signed* _____

   Print Name _____ Print Name _____

PROVIDER ORDERS FOR LIFE-SUSTAINING TREATMENT (POLST)

We call 911 when we have an emergency in most communities. Emergency-response teams come to our aid. Fire fighters and police officers show up at the scene and assess the situation. They begin life-sustaining treatment when needed unless they are otherwise directed. The treatment can include cardiac resuscitation with chest massage, a tube in your airway, and temporary mechanical breathing, if needed.

Many individuals with chronic conditions do not desire such interventions and want to prevent them from happening. This is the situation where a licensed physician, physician's assistant, or nurse practitioner can order full, limited, or no life-sustaining interventions. Your medical provider can order or limit life-sustaining treatment on a form called a POLST (Provider Order for Life-Sustaining Treatment). It will translate your healthcare directive into a medical provider's orders for emergency treatment. It will state what aggressive treatment is to be done and what is not to be done. If there is no POLST order, an emergency crew will do everything they can to keep you alive.

A POLST identifies the individual, their primary-care provider, and the provider's phone number. It has five sections (see attached example).

When a POLST document is completed and signed, it can be copied and placed or carried in a conspicuous place. Emergency responders may have specific instructions for your community. Attach one copy to the DOOR OF YOUR REFRIGERATOR. Carry another copy in your purse or wallet. You might place one in your bedroom in a conspicuous place. Some communities will keep a copy on file at the fire or police department.

Remember, if the emergency responders cannot quickly find your POLST orders, they are required to attempt resuscitation and all other means to keep you alive.

It is wise to review your POLST anytime there is a significant change in your physical condition or you change your living arrangements.

MINNESOTA

Provider Orders for Life-Sustaining Treatment (POLST)

Follow these orders until orders change. These medical orders are based on the patient's current medical condition and preferences. Any section not completed does not invalidate the form and implies full treatment for that section. With significant change of condition new orders may need to be written. Patients should always be treated with dignity and respect.

LAST NAME _____ FIRST NAME _____ MIDDLE INITIAL _____

DATE OF BIRTH _____

PRIMARY MEDICAL CARE PROVIDER NAME _____ PRIMARY MEDICAL CARE PROVIDER PHONE *(WITH AREA CODE)*

A

CHECK ONE

CARDIOPULMONARY RESUSCITATION (CPR) *Patient has no pulse and is not breathing.*

☐ **Attempt** Resuscitation / CPR (Note: selecting this requires selecting "Full Treatment" in Section B).

☐ **Do Not Attempt** Resuscitation / DNR (**Allow Natural Death**).

When not in cardiopulmonary arrest, follow orders in B.

B

CHECK ONE

(NOTE REQUIRE-MENTS)

MEDICAL TREATMENTS *Patient has pulse and/or is breathing.*

☐ **Full Treatment.** Use intubation, advanced airway interventions, and mechanical ventilation as indicated. Transfer to hospital and/or intensive care unit if indicated. All patients will receive comfort-focused treatments.

TREATMENT PLAN: Full treatment including life support measures in the intensive care unit.

☐ **Selective Treatment.** Use medical treatment, antibiotics, IV fluids and cardiac monitor as indicated. No intubation, advanced airway interventions, or mechanical ventilation. May consider less invasive airway support (e.g. CPAP, BiPAP). Transfer to hospital if indicated. Generally avoid the intensive care unit. All patients will receive comfort-focused treatments.

TREATMENT PLAN: Provide basic medical treatments aimed at treating new or reversible illness.

☐ **Comfort-Focused Treatment (Allow Natural Death).** Relieve pain and suffering through the use of any medication by any route, positioning, wound care and other measures. Use oxygen, suction and manual treatment of airway obstruction as needed for comfort. Patient prefers no transfer to hospital for life-sustaining treatments. Transfer if comfort needs cannot be met in current location.

TREATMENT PLAN: Maximize comfort through symptom management.

C

CHECK ALL THAT APPLY

DOCUMENTATION OF DISCUSSION

☐ **Patient** *(Patient has capacity)*   ☐ **Court-Appointed Guardian**   ☐ **Other Surrogate**

☐ **Parent of Minor**   ☐ **Health Care Agent**   ☐ **Health Care Directive**

SIGNATURE OF PATIENT OR SURROGATE

SIGNATURE **(STRONGLY RECOMMENDED)** _____ NAME *(PRINT)* _____

RELATIONSHIP *(IF YOU ARE THE PATIENT, WRITE "SELF")* _____ PHONE *(WITH AREA CODE)* _____

Signature acknowledges that these orders reflect the patient's treatment wishes. Absence of signature does not negate the above orders.

D

SIGNATURE OF PHYSICIAN / APRN / PA

My signature below indicates to the best of my knowledge that these orders are consistent with the patient's current medical condition and preferences.

NAME *(PRINT)* **(REQUIRED)** _____ LICENSE TYPE **(REQUIRED)** _____ PHONE *(WITH AREA CODE)* _____

SIGNATURE **(REQUIRED)** _____ DATE **(REQUIRED)** _____

SEND FORM WITH PATIENT WHENEVER TRANSFERRED OR DISCHARGED. *FAXED, PHOTOCOPIED OR ELECTRONIC VERSIONS OF THIS FORM ARE VALID.*

INFORMATION FOR

HIPAA PERMITS DISCLOSURE TO HEALTH CARE PROVIDERS AS NECESSARY FOR TREATMENT

E | ADDITIONAL PATIENT PREFERENCES *(OPTIONAL)*

CHECK ONE FROM EACH SECTION

ARTIFICIALLY ADMINISTERED NUTRITION *Offer food by mouth if feasible.*

☐ **Long-term artificial nutrition by tube.**

☐ **Defined trial period of artificial nutrition by tube.**

☐ **No artificial nutrition by tube.**

ANTIBIOTICS

☐ **Use IV/IM antibiotic treatment.**

☐ **Oral antibiotics only (no IV/IM).**

☐ **No antibiotics. Use other methods to relieve symptoms when possible.**

ADDITIONAL PATIENT PREFERENCES *(e.g. dialysis, duration of intubation).*

HEALTH CARE PROVIDER WHO PREPARED DOCUMENT

PREPARER NAME *(REQUIRED)*

PREPARER TITLE *(REQUIRED)*

PREPARER PHONE *(WITH AREA CODE)* *(REQUIRED)*

DATE PREPARED *(REQUIRED)*

NOTE TO PATIENTS AND SURROGATES

The POLST form is always voluntary and is for persons with advanced illness or frailty. POLST records your wishes for medical treatment in your current state of health. Once initial medical treatment is begun and the risks and benefits of further therapy are clear, your treatment wishes may change. Your medical care and this form can be changed to reflect your new wishes at any time. However, no form can address all the medical treatment decisions that may need to be made. A Health Care Directive is recommended for all capable adults, regardless of their health status. A Health Care Directive allows you to document in detail your future health care instructions and/or name a Health Care Agent to speak for you if you are unable to speak for yourself.

DIRECTIONS FOR HEALTH CARE PROVIDERS

Completing POLST

- Completing a POLST is always voluntary and cannot be mandated for a patient.
- POLST should reflect current preferences of persons with advanced illness or frailty. Also, encourage completion of a Health Care Directive.
- Verbal / phone orders are acceptable with follow-up signature by physician/APRN/PA in accordance with facility/community policy.
- A surrogate may include a court appointed guardian, Health Care Agent designated in a Health Care Directive, or a person whom the patient's health care provider believes best knows what is in the patient's best interest and will make decisions in accordance with the patient's expressed wishes and values to the extent known, such as a verbally designated surrogate, spouse, registered domestic partner, parent of a minor, or closest available relative.

Reviewing POLST

This POLST should be reviewed periodically, and if:

- The patient is transferred from one care setting or care level to another, or
- There is a substantial change in the patient's health status, or
- The patient's treatment preferences change, or
- The patient's Primary Medical Care Provider changes.

Voiding POLST

- A person with capacity, or the valid surrogate of a person without capacity, can void the form and request alternative treatment.
- Draw line through sections A through E and write "VOID" in large letters if POLST is replaced or becomes invalid.
- If included in an electronic medical record, follow voiding procedures of facility/community.

SEND FORM WITH PATIENT WHENEVER TRANSFERRED OR DISCHARGED. *FAXED, PHOTOCOPIED OR ELECTRONIC VERSIONS OF THIS FORM ARE VALID.*

LAST-HOUR OPTIONS

Many families have had little or no experience with the dying process and are anxious and uncertain. Hospice programs have been superb in making the last months and weeks pleasant and comfortable for all concerned. This is another pitch for entering hospice early during a terminal illness to receive its full benefits. Pain medications, sedatives, and other medications will be administered as needed for comfort. Two other services to consider are an end-of-life doula and compassionate medical-aid-in-dying.

Doulas have been attending childbirth for centuries. They serve the mother as a nonmedical assistant who has valued experience in supporting mothers during labor and birthing. An experienced end-of-life doula can be a valuable addition to assist the patient and family, especially in the final hours. Hospice physicians, nurses, and spiritual leaders provide expertise, but usually do not stay at the bedside for hours and days until the end. But a doula will. They will interpret what is happening and support all the individuals concerned. Medical insurance may or may not cover the cost of a doula.

As we discussed in chapter 13, medical-aid-in-dying is available in several states. Oregon was the first state to allow patients with terminal conditions to take prescription medications that sedate and suppress breathing to bring on death. All states that authorize physicians to prescribe life-ending medications have strict requirements. First, the terminal patient must be in the last six months of expected life. They must be of sound mind, not mentally depressed, and legally capable to make their own decisions. Two physicians, unrelated to the patient, make their evaluations and so certify. One of the physicians writes a lethal prescription that the patient must administer themselves by oral ingestion.

In twenty years, Oregon has had several surprising findings. Many patients who are approved never fill the prescriptions. Just having the option may have relieved their anxiety. There is a significant percentage who fill the prescription but never use it. The families of those who do use the medication to end their lives are almost uniformly supportive and pleased with the process. There has been no rush for this humanitarian service and no political will in the United States to expand it to conditions other than the terminally ill. Having the option of relieving their terminal pain and suffering is comforting in itself.

RESOURCES:

Compassion and Choices
    101 SW Madison Street, #8009
    Portland, OR 97207
    compassionandchoices.org
    phone: 800-247-7421

National End-of-Life Doula Alliance (NEDA)
    P.O. Box 456
    Holderness, NH 03245
    nedalliance.org
    phone: 734-395-9660

International End-of-Life Doula Association (INELDA)
    69 Montgomery St. #287
    Jersey City, NJ 07303
    inelda.org
    phone: 201-540-9049

GRIEF

Grief is a normal human response to the loss of something valuable. Most of us grieve after learning that someone else has a life-threatening disease or injury or dies. But if we are the affected person who wants to go on living, we also will grieve our own impending loss, and our loved ones will share in the loss as bystanders. Grief is an emotion based on the love of one's self or the love of another person. Researchers tell us that love is the basis of all grief.

When we are about to lose someone or something we cherish, we may pass through a cascade of feelings. Elizabeth Kubler-Ross in her seminal book, *On Death and Dying,* first published in 1969, describes five stages of grief starting with denial. She described them presenting sequentially, but we have learned we can start at any stage and move back and forth between stages.

Most of us do not want our lives to end or our loved ones to die. When we receive a terminal diagnosis, we may deny what is happening. When it becomes obvious what is transpiring, we can become angry and frustrated and ask, "Why is this happening?" We may seek more time in a third stage called bargaining. This stage is where intensive medical interventions with surgeries, chemotherapy, radiation, and potent drugs are often used in hopes of adding weeks, months, or years to life for ourselves or our loved ones. It becomes a stage of negotiation where people try to balance the quality-of-life with the prospect of living longer by accepting intensive and extensive treatments that often cause more suffering.

The emotional response can lead to sadness and depression, both in the person directly experiencing the loss and in the loved ones who care for that person. Ideally, everyone associated with the loss reaches a stage, which Kubler-Ross called acceptance. Accepting that the loss is real. Acceptance will give comfort, but it will not prevent the emotional grieving that comes with the loss.

Unfortunately, some individuals get stuck at one of the stages. At one time in the United States, dying patients were not told when they have a disease that is terminal. This practice still continues in some cultures. When patients aren't told the truth by their caregivers, the facade of continuing denial leads to superficial communication and lying at a time when open, honest communication would be beneficial and emotionally more healthy. Patients with a terminal disease often continue futile treatments attempting to bargain for more time, which results in more suffering and added frustration for them and their loved ones.

Accepting your own mortality and bringing your loved ones along is a great gift when it happens. Still, everyone involved will feel the loss and have periods of unexpected and uncontrolled emotions of grief.

There are some things we can do to make the transition better and more tolerable for ourselves and our loved ones. Hospice professionals tell us that a common regret of people dying is they wish that they had told others in their lives how much they meant to them and that they loved them. Dying people also express regret that they did not apologize for something they did or didn't do in the past. Anytime is a good time to seek out those people you may have wronged or hurt and apologize. If you are nearing the end of life, it may be your last chance. Making amends, saying you're sorry, or righting a wrong will relieve the guilt you carry and create a more positive memory for your survivors when you are gone. Tell the people close to you that you love them, and you are grateful they have been part of your life.

Taking these actions may not be easy, but they are likely to be well received and will open up deeper, more rewarding conversations. You will leave a more positive legacy.

What can one do to understand and live with grief after the loss of a loved one? First, accept that it's a normal human emotion to feel sad. Try to engage with other people as much as you can. Talk about your loss with others. You might even join a grief-support group.

Grieving individuals tell us that it can be awkward when friends and relatives say things that make them feel worse. Saying, "I know how you feel," is disingenuous. You can't know how they feel. Saying, "You'll get over it," is another damaging statement. You never get over the loss of a loved one. You learn to move forward, but the memory remains ever present. A more appropriate well wisher might say, "I am sorry for your loss," or, "I love you," or, "I'm holding you in my heart." Instead of asking "What can I do for you?", try to anticipate and fill their immediate needs. Their needs often revolve around food or household chores like lawn mowing, snow shoveling, or other home maintenance.

Many grieving individuals find that doing something for others, such as community volunteering or advocating for an issue, helps them move forward. Continuing with previous habits such as exercising, group activities, or getting together with friends or relatives is important. Grieving persons have told us, "Life is better with people around," and, "Plan ahead. Don't wind up alone."

Herman was a high school teacher and his wife, Elenore, was a family-practice physician. When they retired they decided to stay in the community where their two children lived rather than move to a warmer state like many of their friends. When their house became more of a burden as they aged, they decided to move to a senior apartment where they knew some people and would have fewer responsibilities. They enjoyed the new friendships they made and joined several of the activities in their building. Herman renewed his poker playing and attended regular enrichment lectures.

They both had chronic medical problems, but one day Elenore died unexpectedly. Herman was suddenly faced with being a widower after being married for sixty-two years. He felt bad and wanted to just stay alone in his apartment. His daughter and son were supportive and tried to visit frequently. They all felt sad and missed the woman who had been their wife and mother. Then Herman tried to continue his regular activities. His old and new friends gave him support. Many of his friends had lost spouses, and they talked about their experiences. He says his poker group was particularly helpful. As the weeks and months went by, he said how important his family and friends were for the transition after his wife died.

Elenore and Herman had looked ahead and made thoughtful decisions on where to live and how they wanted to spend their time. Herman was known to say, "We might live to be a 100, but we need a plan." Their wisdom paid off when one of them died. Herman had supportive people around him, who were helpful during his time of grieving.

Dealing with DEMENTIA

Chapter 19

DEMENTIA

Most everyone fears losing their mind. Our mental functions are what make us human. When we have memory lapses we sometimes ask ourselves, "Am I developing Alzheimer's?" "Will my brain function deteriorate so I can no longer care for myself?"

Brain failure like other organ failures can be mild and have little effect on day-to-day life.

It is normal to mislay your eye glasses or to lose your car keys. But when does forgetfulness become abnormal? How do I know that I have the beginnings of the progressive brain disorder we call dementia?

The term dementia is a broad diagnostic category of brain dysfunction that is based on a group of symptoms. They may include a decline in thinking, reasoning, and remembering. Between 60–70 percent of dementia patients have what we know as Alzheimer's disease. Alois Alzheimer was a German pathologist who correlated dementia symptoms to changes he found in the brain of an affected patient. Other less common types of degenerative brain disease causing dementia include Lewy body disease, frontotemporal degeneration, and vascular cognitive impairment caused by a hardening of the arteries that reduces blood flow to the brain. Brain injury from trauma, tumor, or stroke are other causes of dysfunction that can cause symptoms of dementia.

Alzheimer's dementia is a slowly developing process that is associated with amyloid plaques building up in the brain. Despite intensive research, there is no definitive treatment at the time of this writing. Some

73

medications have been shown to temporarily improve some symptoms, but not all patients are able to tolerate the treatments.

There are three broad stages of dementia:

Stage 1. An asymptomatic period where brain changes are taking place without any recognizable symptoms

Stage 2. Mild cognitive impairment where persons may complain of difficulty focusing, of forgetting details of recent events, of missing appointments, of trouble learning new things, of getting lost in once familiar places. They may require notes and written lists as reminders of what they want to do.

Stage 3. Clinical dementia is present when cognitive functions are obviously abnormal. However, the person affected may not be aware that they are not functioning well. Independent living may not be possible at this stage due to difficulties with memory and problem solving.

Clinical Alzheimer's has a progression from mild to moderate to severe disease. Mild symptoms include difficulty remembering, difficulty learning, mood swings, frustrations, confusion, trouble organizing, trouble communicating, and the person may become withdrawn.

Moderate disease is recognized by worsening cognitive functions. Recent memories are lost. The individual requires more help with activities of daily living including food preparation and personal hygiene. He or she may get lost easily.

In severe disease most memory will be absent. Speaking becomes difficult and the individual may need to be fed. They fail to recognize loved ones and become disoriented to place and time of day. Bowel and urine control may be lacking and there is a high risk of falling. Behavior problems may require medication. In late stages mental illness with paranoia and hallucinations may develop.

Diagnosis of Alzheimer's, Lewy body disease and other progressive dementias is mostly based on mental and behavioral symptoms, physical examination to rule out other possibilities, and laboratory and neurological testing. Brain scans and spinal-fluid analysis can be helpful, but only post-mortem examination of a patient's brain can confirm a specific diagnosis.

There are some activities that have been associated with reduced incidence or delay of the onset of progressive dementias: regular aerobic exercise, a Mediterranean diet high in vegetables and unsaturated oils, good cardiovascular health, adequate sleep, and mental activity, especially new learning. The amount invested into dementia research enhances the prospect for more targeted treatments in the future.

Caring for someone with dementia is more than a one-person job. Asking for and organizing help is one of the most important things a caregiver can do. The caregiver can find help in books, videos, instructional meetings, and participation in support groups.

Most communities have some resources for managing dementia. Contact professionals like primary medical-care physicians and assistants, geriatric-care specialists, social workers, insurance company case managers, and faith-community nurses.

Other services that may be needed include transportation, food services like Meals-on-Wheels, legal and financial services, adult daycare services, respite care for the caregiver, home health care, household services, assisted-living or skilled-nursing-home care.

The prospect of caring for someone who shows signs of deteriorating mental function can seem overwhelming. Finding another person who has had experience dealing with dementia caregiving can be rewarding. Knowing someone to talk to or finding a peer through a support organization will help. A trusted sympathetic listener who is willing to just listen can be essential to the well-being of a dementia caregiver.

RESOURCES:

Alzheimer's Association. https://alz.org, 1-800-272-3900

BrightFocus Foundation. http://www.brightfocus.org, 1-855-345-6237

Mace, Nancy L. and Rabins, Peter V. *The 36-Hour Day: A Family Guide to Caring for People Who Have Alzheimer Disease, Other Dementias, and Memory Loss.* Baltimore, MD: Johns Hopkins Press, 2017.

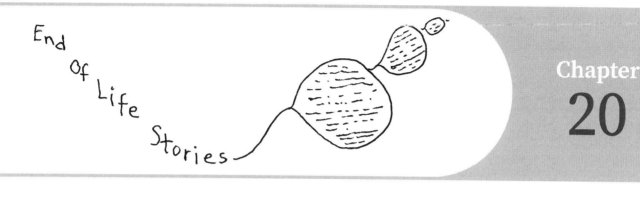

END-OF-LIFE STORIES

Arnie and his wife, Fern, who we met in Chapter 14, were in their eighties when they completed healthcare directives, gave copies to their adult children, to their physicians, and they discussed their wishes with their immediate family. They both requested medical treatments unless there was little hope for meaningful recovery. In that case they wished to be made comfortable and not be kept alive by artificial means. They trusted their healthcare agents to make medical decisions, if they could not make them for themselves.

Arnie was in his early nineties when he developed a cough, shortness of breath, and often became confused. He was thought to have an early pneumonia superimposed on chronic respiratory failure, which led to hospitalization. His healthcare directive had not been updated for many years. Fern, who was his designated healthcare agent, said, "He didn't want to be kept alive on machines, but he did want to be treated with medications and oxygen."

His chest X-ray hadn't changed but his oxygen concentration was very low. He was started on antibiotics, breathing treatments, and oxygen. He also had been in treatment for metastatic prostate cancer.

Over the next five days his mental status improved and he began having conversations with his doctors and family. He wanted to remove the oxygen therapy, which he was receiving through a small tube at each nasal opening. His attending physician was called, and a bedside family conference was arranged. The doctor explained that the oxygen was keeping him alive and without it he might die. Arnie said, "Let's try it."

The doctor went over the situation again and emphasized the need for continuing the oxygen. Arnie said he understood and still wanted the oxygen stopped. As the doctor left the room to write the order, Arnie said, "Remember."

The doctor turned back and asked, "Remember what?"

"Remember what we talked about."

The oxygen was removed, and Arnie's breathing became more labored and the delirium returned. He received comfort medications, and died peacefully three days later with his family by his side.

Arnie is an example of someone who had completed a healthcare directive, discussed his wishes with his family, and had designated a healthcare agent to make decisions when he was disabled. When his mental condition improved he consciously made the decision to withdraw his oxygen therapy even though he knew it would likely end his life.

Lillian was in her eighties when she had a severe stroke that required life support to keep her alive. The attending physicians felt she had little chance of meaningful recovery. She was unable to communicate her wishes, and it was up to her family to make decisions on how to proceed. She and her husband had healthcare directives that named their eldest son as their agent. When the doctors presented the situation to the family members who lived nearby, there was agreement that continuing life support was not what what she would have wanted. But their third and youngest son, who lived in another state, had not been included in their healthcare-directive discussions due to the inconvenience of travel. When the family convened with the doctors, he was not ready to remove life support and argued strongly to keep his mother alive. The husband and other two sons wanted the family to be united in the decisions that needed to be made. The disagreement went on for hours and created major emotional reactions. Eventually they all agreed to remove life-support measures and allow nature to take its course. She died several days later, but some of the emotional scars remain years later.

Lillian was not able to make her own decisions when a life-threatening condition developed. She had a written healthcare directive and a son had agreed to be her agent. But not all of the family had been involved in the earlier discussions. When the acute situation developed, there was disagreement within the family about removing life-support measures. This example emphasizes the importance of including all the significant family members in conversations about end-of-life planning. Excluding one of the sons led to a family conflict at a critical time and caused an unpleasant memory that could have been avoided.

Carol was in her mid-nineties when she expressed to her son's family that she did not want life-sustaining medical treatment, if necessary, when she could not make decisions for herself. She lived independently in a senior apartment with minimal medical problems until her ninety-ninth year when she began falling for no apparent reason. Medical evaluation found that her heart would stop for up to thirty seconds at a time. The heart node that initiates her heartbeat was wearing out. She had no serious injuries from her falls, but she was at great risk of passing out due to lack of blood flow to her brain when her heart had no effective beat for a period of time lasting more that ten seconds. The heart specialist recommended a pacemaker and explained the limited surgical procedure. She and her family had planned to refuse all life- sustaining treatment. Now she was faced with living a bed-to-chair existence in a nursing home or having a pacemaker that would allow her to return to living independently in her apartment. She changed her mind about medical intervention and decided to have a pacemaker surgically placed. Her heart responded well to the pacemaker, and she went home the next day to her apartment. Subsequently she moved to another state to be closer to her son's family where she died in her 100th year.

Carol changed her mind when a-life-threatening situation developed. Fortunately she was able to make the decision for herself. Once a healthcare directive is documented, filed, and communicated to important people, it still can be changed as Carol's example shows us. Her decision allowed her to get back to her apartment and to move her residence to be closer to her family.

Helena was a widow in her late seventies when her family noted her memory was slipping. She was living alone in the home where she and her husband had raised a large family. At the urging of her adult children, she accepted a move to an assisted-living facility in the same city. Gradually her mental functioning declined in spite of her participation in clinical trials for Alzheimer's disease at a local university. The decade decline eventually led to a bed-to-chair life in a skilled nursing home.

Helena did have a healthcare directive completed before she began her mental decline. She did not want to be kept alive by artificial means if there was no hope of meaningful recovery. This gave her family comfort and allowed them to discuss how they should treat her as the end approached. She had designated a son-in-law to be her healthcare agent.

In her last year she was less responsive and had to be fed. She began having trouble swallowing and was choking on liquids. Eventually, she stopped eating. Her family decided to offer food and thickened liquids but not to force-feed her.

Her extended family was in agreement that artificially extending her life was not in her best interests. Comfort care and medications were ordered and antibiotics were withheld when she developed a low-grade fever from either an aspiration pneumonia or a urinary-tract infection.

She slipped into a coma, and her family realized the end was near. Several grandchildren began to make plans to visit her, some from distant parts of the country. A memorial service was planned for a Sunday afternoon when all the family would be together. All six of her children and twelve of her thirteen grandchildren were planning to come.

Her breathing was labored on that Sunday morning, but she was still alive. That afternoon the memorial service in the nursing-home chapel went on as planned. Family and friends reminisced about her life and what she had meant to them. Readings from her bedside notebook brought her voice into the celebration.

A buffet meal was served, pictures were taken, and family connections were renewed. Then, as evening was coming, members of the family began moving to her bedside to hold her cooling hands and to tell her they loved her. The collection of people trailed into the hallway as individuals moved to her bedside to say their final good-byes. There were twenty-one individuals nearby when she took her last breath.

Helena had dementia that had gradually worsened since she had signed her healthcare directive a decade earlier. She was not competent to make decisions when she developed what appeared to be a life-threatening infection. Her family wanted her to be comfortable but were not wishing to prolong an illness that had left her unable to communicate or to safely eat or drink without choking. Her children were all in agreement that further prolonging her life with medical interventions was not what she would have wanted. The ten-year-old document stating she did not want to be kept alive if there was no hope of recovery was a comfort to all concerned.

PART THREE

Our Legacies

Thinking of Legacies

OUR LEGACIES

As we go through life we are creating our stories. Our activities and actions add up to what others see as our character and our personal contributions. As we approach the later years of life many of us begin to think about what we will be leaving behind when our earthly life ends. In other words, what will be our legacies?

Loved ones will remember us. Some will grieve our leaving and mourn their loss. Those closest to us may want to organize a memorial or a funeral service to recognize our passing.

Someone will need to disperse our personal property, real estate, and settle our financial accounts. When a physician says, "It's time to get your affairs in order," it may be too late to do it thoughtfully. We recommend not waiting for a crisis. Plan ahead while you have the time and energy to do the task well.

The next seven chapters are the actions we should consider. Most of us think of our financial affairs such as bank accounts, investment accounts, personal property, real estate, and estate-planning first. We may be thinking of bequests to charities and distribution of family keepsakes. But there are other important things we can do to make the lives of our survivors easier, and more rewarding. We can write letters to our family about our love for them and the values we wish to pass on. We can state what is important to us if we are unable to make our wishes known. What sort of memorial or funeral service, if any, do we want? Where are our important papers stored? We can communicate our wishes with our loved ones and designated agents. The people we leave behind will be grateful that we took the time and made the effort to consciously plan our legacies.

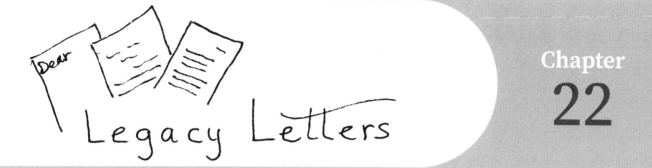

LEGACY LETTERS

What would you like your family to remember about you? Writing letters to important people in your life is one way to transmit your thoughts and to leave a lasting impression. A written letter is an opportunity to tell people you love them and what values and beliefs you would like to pass on as a lasting remembrance. A letter is another vehicle to apologize and resolve some conflicts or regrets. Speaking to someone directly is worthwhile, but putting your heartfelt feelings in written form can be more effective and durable. You may also choose to have a conversation, especially if you want to open a discussion and get feedback. But a letter can become a keepsake, something cherished long after you are gone.

Who might be a recipient of such a letter and how to begin? Think about the important people in your life. Tell them you are proud of them and what they have accomplished. Express gratitude for having had them in your life. Express your affection and what you would like them to remember about you. Reflect on the meaningful experiences and values you have shared.

Healthcare professionals who work with people nearing the end of life talk about how many of their patients have regrets. Making apologies for any transgressions or omissions you have made in your life to other people will enhance their remembrance of you. In effect, settling past accounts is part of a good estate plan and one that many people overlook.

Legacy letters can go by many names: family letters, ethical wills, ethical writings, etc. They connect you to the next generation of family and friends. They preserve the memory of your life, your values, and your wisdom. Writing from your heart can be rewarding for you and will be appreciated. Writing such a letter can be an opportunity to celebrate life and to make a difference in the lives of others.

How do you get started? Rachael Freed in her book, *Your Legacy Matters,* outlines a one-page letter. She says to take no more than fifteen minutes for a first draft. The first paragraph should state what the letter is about. Explain you are writing now because we don't know what the future will bring, and you want to share some of the values and wisdom you have learned from your experiences.

In the second paragraph tell a story or stories that were meaningful to you. In a third paragraph reflect on the meaning of what you want to pass on from the story or stories. In the fourth paragraph close with why you wrote the letter, your willingness to discuss it further, and end with a statement to future generations.

Your letter may be addressed to anyone. Many of us start with our spouses, children, or close friends. There may be others that you wish to acknowledge or with whom to make amends. You may want to write a "last letter" to be opened after you die.

Our advice: don't die with regrets you can overcome while alive. If you can, write in longhand and date the letter. If you don't send the letter immediately, you can revise it later.

Some individuals write periodic letters to people in their families. One person we know writes a letter to each new grandchild on their first birthday. Many people write an autobiography and print it in a pamphlet. Occasionally someone will publish a book to become a family heirloom. But often writing a 15-minute letter is more likely to get finished and sent than a book that never gets completed.

When Steve hit the pivotal age of sixty-five, he wrote a letter to his children about what gave meaning to his life. Later, when he contemplated retirement, he wrote another letter about how he had approached his work. When he actually retired, he began writing down the stories he and his wife had experienced. Some of the stories were published. Eventually he collected these stories in a book he said was for the children of his grandson to read in their old age. He said it was a letter his great-grandfather wrote to his family that got him started.

RESOURCES:

Freed, Rachael. *Your Legacy Matters: A Multi-Generational Guide for Writing Your Ethical Will*. Minerva Press, 2013.

"The Stanford Letter Project" Periyakoil, V.J., https://www.med.stanford.edu/letter.html

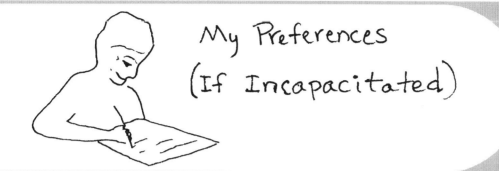

My Preferences
(If Incapacitated)

WHAT'S IMPORTANT TO ME?

There may come a time when we are unable to manage our day-to-day lives and will need to rely on others to help us. We may be unable to tell our caregivers what we want or even what we need. None of us looks forward to such a day, but let's think about the possibility and document what we might want.

What is most important for your loved ones and caregivers to know about you? We all have different preferences that bring us pleasure and joy. Write these down before we become incapacitated.

Alma was ninety-one years old when she was transferred to a nursing home after suffering a stroke. The stroke left her unable to speak and to use her right arm and leg. The transfer information from the hospital noted she had been living alone since her husband died twenty years ago. She was said to be childless, and no one had visited during her twelve-day hospital stay. There were many medical reports from her hospitalization: including X-rays, scans, lab reports, consultations, and medical summaries. But there was no information about her life before her stroke other than she was a widow with no known relatives, and she lived independently on her social security income.

Her rehabilitation at the nursing home did not progress well. In fact over the first month she seemed to be getting weaker, more curled up and less responsive. She had her eyes closed most of the day; she had to be fed; and she was losing weight. The physical and occupational therapists could not get her to actively participate in any of their therapies or social activities.

At a weekly care conference the social worker was asked if he had any ideas or anything to offer. He said he would try to see if he could learn something about her background. He soon realized this woman had no recorded social history in her medical records aside from living alone. Her stroke had limited her ability to communicate and she was regressing and becoming more disabled six weeks into her illness. He was able to contact one of her neighbors. Alma was known in her neighborhood as a recluse, and none of her neighbors even knew she was ill. They thought she had moved or was out of town. Her closest neighbor, who had lived next door for seven years, thought at one time Alma had played an instrument in the local symphony orchestra, but she had no other information.

The social worker contacted the current orchestra director who didn't know Alma, but he had the phone number of the previous director who was retired. The retired director did remember Alma as a devoted violist. She had sat first chair in the viola section most of the years he was director. He had not seen or heard from her, for over twenty years. He remembered she retired when her husband became terminally ill and seemed to drop all her community connections after that.

The social worker brought a tape player and some classical-music tapes into Alma's room one sunny afternoon and began to play a Beethoven symphony. Alma opened her eyes, looked at him, and smiled. It was her first positive interaction in over a month.

Alma seemed to brighten anytime the music was played. The staff played music in her room most of the day and brought in additional tapes. Alma indicated she knew most of the pieces and began directing the music with her good arm. She began taking an active part in her physical-strengthening and occupational therapies. Soon she was feeding herself and going to the dining room. She learned to make herself understood even though her speech remained limited. She gradually made a satisfactory adjustment to her disabilities, had music coming from her room most of day, and was eventually able to be transported to live concerts and other excursions. She required skilled-nursing services indefinitely, but now her caregivers competed to be assigned to her music-filled room.

We present Alma's story to emphasize the importance of having someone know what is important to you, if at some time you cannot make your wishes known to the people who are caring for you. Put what matters to you down on paper or in a recording for your loved ones and caregivers.

THINK ABOUT WHAT MATTERS TO YOU

Write in the spaces below or write a letter for your family, friends, and medical provider. Ask them to read it and save it while you are alive.

- Daily activities, routines, pleasures that make life enjoyable and interesting

- Hobbies, and other interests such as music or art

- People, pets, places, or possessions that are important to you

- Accomplishments and personal stories that give a picture of your life

- Personal values and spiritual beliefs

- Other things that are important to you

RESOURCES:

"Stanford Letter Project," Periyakoil,V. J., https://www.med.stanford .edu/letter.html

Carol Stephens, Psy.D, LP, CBSM, Stephens Psychological Services, SPS@hushmail.com

MONEY AND PROPERTY

As we age our financial needs and requirements change. Those of us who have retired have ceased accumulating investment dollars for retirement and have started to use them for living expenses. If we have achieved a desirable lifestyle, we can begin to think about what else we wish to do with our money and property. We can keep what we have and let our estate fall to our heirs when we die. Or we can make gifts to our family, friends, or charities while we are living.

Depending on your situation you might hire a financial advisor, an accountant, or a lawyer to help you make sound decisions. Our discussion here is meant to stimulate your thoughts and discussions with your family and advisors. We are not supplying financial advice or any legal opinions.

The federal and state governments allow transfer of money and property tax free within specified limits. The federal government in 2021 allows a person to give up to $15,000 to as many individuals as we want. A married couple can give a maximum of $30,000 to each beneficiary free of taxes. For families wishing to pass financial assets to the next generation, this is a good place to start. One caution: if your holdings consist of stocks or bonds that have appreciated in value in a taxable account, any sale will lead to capital-gain taxes while you are living. If the assets are to pass to your heirs after your death, there will be a "step up in basis" and any capital gain will be eliminated. It is always best to consult your financial advisors before making any gifts.

Passing down a property is more complicated, but it is possible. Seek expert advice. Some complicated transactions can be done by individuals who are willing to spend the time and energy to learn the intricacies of ownership transfers. Still, the cost of engaging a professional expert can give one peace of mind and prevent unwanted complications.

There are several advantages to passing down some of your financial or real estate assets while you are living. Depending on your total assets and where you live, you can lower or eliminate estate taxes when you die. The estate-tax laws frequently change, which is another good reason to seek professional advice.

A second reason is that your heirs will be thankful to have extra unrestricted resources at their disposal. Giving while you are living rather than dividing up all of your estate after death is usually satisfying for the giver also.

Charities appreciate any gifts at the time they are given. You can plan to make charitable contributions at your death. They are called bequests or future planned gifts. The charities appreciate being notified whenever you decide on a planned gift. State and federal tax considerations can be an incentive for some donors to make their charitable giving while they are living. Gifts up to $100,000 given directly from an IRA retirement plan to a federally qualified 501(c)3 charity currently is considered a Qualified Charitable Distribution and not an income item for the taxpayer. No taxes will be owed when funds are distributed directly from an IRA to a qualified charity. Financial gifts can get complicated for the general taxpayer and expert advice is highly recommended.

There is another benefit of charitable giving while you are able. Your living heirs will not be conflicted between what they receive and what a charity receives at your death. They will divide all of what is left of your estate. It is important to have a conversation about your intentions. It will avoid any second-guessing later. Giving to family and charities while still living is not for everybody, but is is something to think about when planning what to do with your estate.

How do we know if we have enough resources to last our expected lifetime? If a person has a terminal illness and has been admitted to hospice, the calculation is not hard. But if we are reasonably well, with no known risk factors except our age, we can consult life-expectancy tables. Then estimate our yearly expenses (including taxes and inflation). Multiply estimated yearly expenses by expected life expectancy and you have the minimum you need for yourself. Then add to the total any unusual expenses such as a move, residence purchase, etc. The result is an estimate of your expected lifetime expenses. Most of us would feel more comfortable with a cushion, such as adding five or even ten years of living expenses to the calculation.

Next, you need to estimate your expected income. Add up the income from fixed sources such as social security, annuities, private company retirement plans, and required distributions from IRAs and other government-qualified plans, and any other sources. The difference between your expected annual expenses and your expected income will be the amount you add to or need to withdraw from your investment principle. Taking time to put pen to paper with this exercise can help you decide if giving to family or charities is feasible. The alternative is to designate a specific dollar amount, a percentage of your estate, or a specific property to be given at your death. Giving while living can be rewarding if your expected income and expenses are secure.

Stan and Jean worked as professionals in the healthcare and education fields. They were nearly the same age. Jean retired in her late fifties to pursue other interests. Stan kept working until his mid-seventies, reducing his workload the last decade. They both started receiving social security payments in their sixties and had minimal withdrawals from their retirement funds until Stan retired.

As Stan and Jean approached the end of their seventies, they looked at their income and expenses and found they were only taking the required minimum distributions from their retirement plans. They sold their townhouse and moved to a rental apartment. When they thought about the decades to come, they felt secure that their income from social security and retirement plans would last well beyond their life expectancy and their spending needs and wants. That was when their accountant and tax advisor suggested they consider passing down some of their money to their heirs. The younger family members were well established adults, but had long-term debt that eventually needed to be paid off. They were ready to begin paying off their debt early, so Stan and Jean began transferring a sum of money from their estate to family members each year.

Next they took an offer from a charitable foundation where Stan worked to seriously delve into estate planning. While their estate was modest, it was more than they needed, and they wanted to plan some giving to their favorite charities. They decided that they would donate about

10 percent of their net worth to educational and religious institutions where they had relationships. They realized it could be twenty years or more before a bequest to a charity would be received. The institutions were glad to have written bequest pledges for their files, but also requested annual contributions for operations.

Stan and Jean gave some of their money to support education scholarships. They were able to meet some of the early recipients and were gratified to see the early results of their donations.

There are many ways to enrich the lives of others besides financial contributions. Giving of your time and talents is as important as giving financial support to your family and charities. Each of us has to decide how, what, and when to give. Many of us find joy and satisfaction when we enhance the lives of others.

Financial — Representative

FINANCIAL REPRESENTATIVES

We all like to be independent, especially when it comes to our finances. However, there may come a time when we are unable to make important financial decisions. At that time another person will have the legal authority to make financial decisions for you. That person of your choosing will be designated as your financial agent, much like your designated healthcare agent as described in chapter 13. The law calls this person an attorney of fact who will have the durable power of attorney. This is a temporary authority and can be rescinded on your recovery. Take the time to carefully appoint this important position. If you do not appoint a financial agent, your spouse, your children, or legal next of kin will make financial decisions for you. States have differing laws that go into effect if you do not designate a financial agent. Your financial agent must look out for you and your heirs' best interests. If a state court has to appoint an agent, you or your estate may incur unnecessary expenses.

The next chapters will discuss wills and financial planning at the end of life. The executor of your will is another person you need to designate. He or she will have the power to sell and distribute your property according to the directions in your will. It is important to talk to the person or persons you choose for this important role to establish their willingness to assume the responsibility.

Selecting your financial agent and the executor of your will requires care. The person for each role should be someone you fully trust to act in your best interests. One person could serve both roles if you wish. Most advisors suggest you avoid having co-agents for either role. Co-agents require both persons to sign every action and may require both to be present especially when closing accounts or selling property. Select persons who will not be swayed by emotions or pressures from people who may want your assets distributed in a way contrary to your wishes as stated in your will. Some individuals will choose a spouse or a child. Others will choose a neutral party like a lawyer or an institution like a bank. The person you choose has a legal obligation to carry out your wishes as expressed in your will. The executor will also transfer and distribute your assets after your death and file your last tax return.

Have in-depth conversations with your financial agents for them to understand the specifics of your wishes and to know exactly where your financial records are kept. Tell your agents all your account locations, account numbers, passwords, and the contact information of people who will need to be consulted.

Some words of caution for anyone asked to be an executor of an estate. Being an executor is no small task. The executor of large estates may spend hundreds of hours and possibly many years at this job. Executors can draw a reasonable fee for their services from the estate.

As executor you will need to track down all the individual's assets. Some assets such as real estate or artwork may require appraisals. Outstanding bills and other creditors will need to be paid. Tax returns will need to be filed and whatever remains will need to be distributed to the heirs. You can hire experts to help, but ultimately the legal (fiduciary) responsibility is yours. As long as the heirs are amenable to the executor's decisions the process will move forward. But if there are disputes that lead to court battles, the process could drag on for years. Ultimately, an executor could be sued by one or more of the beneficiaries. Establishing a dialogue with the heirs and keeping them informed during the process can help prevent misunderstandings and head off potential conflicts. The executor may need to hire legal advisors.

Being an executor of an estate is a significant responsibility. Anyone considering taking on such a task should think carefully about whether they are prepared to commit the time and energy to the process. Be prepared and willing to seek expert advice when you sense you are getting beyond your capabilities or need a second opinion.

Alfred's mother-in-law, whom I will call Angela, was urged to update her healthcare directive and will after her husband died. She was in good health but nearing eighty years old, and her family wished to be assured she would have enough resources to continue her lifestyle and maintain the family home. They had also noticed Angela was starting to have memory lapses.

Her lawyer scheduled a meeting, asked her to bring a list of her financial holdings, an estimate of her annual expenses, and to bring the family members she wanted to be part of the decision making. Alfred and his wife were asked to attend the meeting.

During the meeting the lawyer explained what needed to be done. As part of the process he recommended she choose a healthcare agent to be responsible for making healthcare decisions if she was incapacitated and could not make them for herself. She turned to Alfred since he was a healthcare professional and he agreed. Next the lawyer said she needed to select an executor—someone who would be in charge of carrying out the provisions of her will after she died. Again she turned to Alfred. He was surprised and wondered if one of her children might be a more logical choice. She was insistent that it was Alfred whom she wanted. He thought about it another day and talked it over with some of the other family members before he contacted the attorney the next day and agreed.

After a few weeks the attorney scheduled another meeting to sign her healthcare directive, the will, and power-of-attorney papers. Alfred received copies. When filing the copies away, he noted his mother-in-law had listed the funds in her brokerage account and her house and contents as her only assets.

One day about three years later Angela's broker called Alfred and requested a meeting in his office. He had noted the some of Angela's financial holdings were being signed over to a family member to be used as collateral. Alfred and his wife knew that family members had borrowed money from their parents over the years while their father was alive. Now another family member was borrowing money, and Angela's broker was concerned that she did not understand what she was doing.

Alfred and his wife began reviewing the brokerage transactions and searching for any family records. They gradually pieced together an incomplete history of family loans and repayments over the last twenty years. It turned out than many family members had taken out family loans for real estate or business purposes. Some repayments were noted in an account book, but some of the book's pages were missing.

At this point Alfred felt he needed expert advice and enlisted the lawyer who had written Angela's will. The lawyer and Alfred sent letters to the identified borrowers asking them to come forward with their understanding of whether the outstanding funds were a loan or to be considered a gift. Not everyone responded. Those that did were able to work out a repayment plan. No one said the money was a gift. Those who did not respond were given an estimate of what Alfred could document that they owed. He informed them that that amount would be deducted from any future inheritance unless repaid.

Years passed and Angela needed to move to an assisted-living facility and eventually to a nursing home. Alfred had to sell her house, which needed repair. He had to hire contractors to fix the roof, refinish the floors, and repaint the house inside and outside. When the house sold he had to invest the funds that now formed the bulk of her assets. He also had to pay her medical and nursing-home bills and file her taxes each year. Alfred had been responsible for her finances for ten years before her death. Over the years all her assets had been moved to one financial institution. After all the bills were paid and taxes filed, the remaining assets needed to be distributed to the legal heirs. The heirs with documented outstanding loans had their inheritance reduced by their residual loan balances. Not everyone was pleased, but the majority agreed it was fair.

Alfred said he had no idea what a long and involved process that he as a healthcare and executor would be undertaking. He said the one thing that gave him confidence was hiring legal advisors when needed.

WILLS

A will is a legal document that allows you to transfer your money, personal belongings, and any other property you may own to others who survive you. It is an important document and can get complicated. The discussion here is meant to present some general information and cannot be taken as advice or specific recommendations. You can think of your will as the foundation of your legacy planning.

There is no law that requires you to have a will, but anyone with significant financial assets, real estate ownership, or personal property, including automobiles, is wise to take the time and effort to legally secure this part of your legacy. If you don't have a will and have no spouse, the state in which you live may distribute your assets by that state's heirship formula. Even if you have a trust, life-insurance policies with named beneficiaries, or joint ownership of real estate or bank accounts, it is still recommended that you have a viable will for your specific intentions.

You can write your own will as long as you follow the rules of your state. In most states you must be of legal age. The will must be in writing and be signed by you or by another person at your direction and in your presence, or by a court-appointed representative. In most states your signature must be witnessed by one or more persons. Most people with significant assets hire an attorney who will assure adherence to all the state laws and rules.

Your will names your spouse, if married, living children, and the other beneficiaries you choose. It will tell your will executor how you want your residual assets passed to your heirs after your final expenses, debts, and taxes are paid. You can designate tangible personal property—items that can be touched, felt, or moved—that you wish to give to specific persons or charities such as vehicles, furniture, artwork, jewelry, etc. A list of the items and the recipients can be attached to your basic will document.

The will names your personal representative (executor) and your successors and their financial responsibilities. If you have created trusts, the will gives direction to the trustee(s). Many wills designate a percentage of remaining assets to go to survivors or charities. The will contains the name and contact information for your personal representative (executor) who will manage the estate. It will contain additional specific information such as any trusts created, names of a guardian for any minor children, and an alternative guardian if your first choice is unable or unwilling to act. The document must be signed by you and by witnesses.

In preparing your will you need to inventory your assets and your debts (if any) and decide specifically how you want the remaining assets to be distributed. There are tax-efficient methods of transferring assets on a person's death that are not available otherwise. Most of us benefit from the advice of a financial counselor or a tax attorney. The process can get complicated and the designation of beneficiaries and trusts can make a big difference in the amount transferred to your heirs and the amount paid to the governments in taxes.

The person you name to be your representative must be a person you trust to carry out your wishes. He or she will pay any debts you may have, pay any taxes you owe, file your final tax returns, and distribute any remaining assets according to your designations. This is a legal fiduciary role, and he or she will be held to a high standard of care in dealing with your estate.

It is important to clearly state who is to get your property when you die. It should indicate how much or what percent of the estate should go to each person or charity named. Personal property should be itemized and organized so your agent can make the required distributions.

You can change your will at any time. But you must do it by making a new will or amending the old one with an attachment, called a codicil. A codicil must clearly state the changes to the original and it must be signed and witnessed in the same way as the original will. You can add another level of authenticity called self-proving the will. A will is self-proved when you and two witnesses state in affidavits that you executed the will voluntarily, were of required age, were not under undue influence, and were of sound mind. A will can be self-proved at the time it is executed or any time thereafter. This adds another level of authenticity and helps establish that your will will be properly executed in case it is contested in court.

Your will and itemized list distributing your possessions should be reviewed and updated periodically. The original will and any codicils should be kept together and located with your important papers.

Many of us start giving our heirlooms to our family while we are living. Household items and items of emotional value, that have minimal financial value, can conveniently be passed along at any time. Items of significant value can be gifted to any person as described in chapter 24. Our experience with families suggest this can be accomplished as long as the heirs feel they are treated fairly. The best way to avoid conflict is to do any gifting to heirs as equally as possible.

ESTATE PLANNING, TRUSTS, AND PROBATE

Most of us have some possessions that legally comprise our estate. We use our possessions for our own and our loved ones' benefit while living. At some time during our lives or after we die, we will want those possessions to be distributed to family, friends, or charities. Without a plan, our resources may not last our lifetime. Without a plan a government representative will decide how they are distributed during a process called probate. The purpose of estate planning is to assure your spending will last your expected life span; any residual property will be distributed to people and charities you designate; and government taxes will be minimized.

A well-planned will is the basis for an effective estate plan. Anyone who has a regular job, has any savings or investments, or any debt such as car or mortgage payments, should have a will. We discussed making your will in the last chapter. Planning what you wish to accomplish financially over the rest of your life and beyond is the purpose of this chapter.

Things to consider:

1. Will my savings and investments last my lifetime? Do I need to reduce my spending? Can I afford to spend more on things like travel or gifting? Do I know how much expendable income I have each year? Do I know how much I spend? Is there a

surplus or a deficit? Rough calculations with pencil and paper will suffice. Note the sources of income and debt.

2. Who do I wish to benefit from any property I have now or might have in the future? Think of your spouse, children, parents, relatives, other persons, and charities.

3. Create a list of all the properties you own or expect to own, including their approximate value. Besides real estate and personal property, the list should include all bank and investment accounts, any life-insurance policies, retirement plans, and their location and identifying account numbers.

4. Consider how you wish to have your estate passed down to your heirs. Do you wish them to receive property or income? How will the federal and state tax laws affect your decisions?

5. Do I have the professional assistance I need to make good decisions? Think about consulting attorneys, accountants, investment advisors, trust officers, insurance professionals, or real estate brokers. Not everyone will need all these specialists to develop an effective, efficient, and legal plan.

The main building blocks after writing a will are establishing trusts. A will and trusts are the tools for making an effective estate plan. Your will lays out distribution of any possession not covered by trusts, joint ownerships, or other plans.

Trusts have many uses. Trusts are often created to minimize taxes and to avoid probate courts. When one spouse dies, all the couples' assets flow to the surviving spouse if no other provisions have been made, and usually no estate taxes will be due. When the second person dies, the remaining estate may be taxed depending on its value. In 2021 the federal estate tax excludes the first $11 million in assets. Most of us will not be concerned about the federal estate taxation, but we should know about our state estate-tax laws. Some states have no estate taxes. Others follow the federal rules. But many states have estate taxes that exclude much less than the federal government. It is important for you to know the approximate value of your estate and the inheritance laws of your state of residence. These limits change over time. You might need professional advice to understand the implications of estate taxes on how much of your estate will pass to your heirs and how much will be taken by state and federal governments.

When you create a revocable trust you are giving the trustee the authority to make financial decisions within the trust. You can name yourself as the initial trustee, but a successor trustee will be required in case you are incapacitated or die. The trustee and successor trustee should be people or institutions you trust to make decisions in your and your heirs' best interests and to carry out your stated wishes.

The main advantage of a revocable trust is that the trustee can distribute the assets to the designated heirs in your will without involving probate courts, which saves time and avoids legal costs. The second advantage is that the trust can be revoked should your needs or situation change.

Not every financial asset can be put in a trust. Common transfers include real estate, personal properties such as cars and boats, and taxable bank and investment accounts. On the other hand federally qualified retirement accounts, such as IRAs and 401(k)s, cannot be moved to a revocable trust. Seek expert advice in sorting out the advantages of trusts, designating beneficiaries, and designating ownership of financial accounts and real estate.

Trusts are used for many other purposes. A trust can also be managed to provide income to one or more minor children or disabled persons for a defined period of time and then be paid out at a defined age. Trusts also are used to avoid probate-court proceedings.

Sylvia was a single parent with a terminal disease. She wanted to ensure that her children would have adequate financial resources until they finished their education, at which time they would receive the bulk of a significant trust fund. She also wanted to be sure they were mature enough to manage the money themselves when they received the trust payout.

Sylvia created a trust for each child and contracted with the bank's trust department to manage and invest the funds. She authorized a monthly sum for the support of each child and education support at the trustee's discretion. She decided that they should have full access to the trust when they were twenty-eight. She chose twenty-eight because that was the age when she and her husband finished their education, were married, and wanted to buy a house.

Karolin was a single parent whose husband had died accidentally in his early thirties.

She had one developmentally delayed daughter who was not expected to become a fully functioning adult. Karolin arranged a trust for her daughter through a bank that would contain all her assets when she died. When Karolin died, a guardian was appointed for the daughter by a state court as designated in her will. The bank trustees sold her house and car and moved all her financial assets into a trust. Karolin designated family heirlooms to other heirs should their value not be needed to support her daughter. Eventually the trust funds diminished to the point where the heirlooms were appraised and the designated heirs were asked if they wished to purchase the items, which they did. When the trust funds were finally depleted, the guardian and the state court authorized state support until the daughter died of natural causes in her seventies.

We told the long story of Alfred and his mother-in-law's estate when we discussed choosing financial representatives in chapter 25. When she died, Alfred said the trust she set up worked perfectly. With the death certificate he could close her bank and investment accounts, notify social security and an annuity company, and pay out the remaining assets to her heirs according to her will. Probate court was completely avoided, and the final process was completed in less than six weeks.

These examples are only some of the ways trusts can aid in distributing assets after death. Trusts can be complex and most require expert consultation to obtain their full benefit. Working with an estate-planning professional will be money well spent and will give you the peace of mind that you are not leaving loose ends for your loved ones to sort out after you are gone.

Making Memorial/Funeral Plans

MEMORIAL AND FUNERAL PLANNING

Planning your own funeral may sound morbid to some people, but it is an important gift that you can leave your loved ones. Thinking through what you want and making definite plans can relieve some of your concerns toward the end of life. Once you have made plans for your burial, cremation, or body donation, it is important to tell your loved ones your plans. You will be giving direction to your survivors at an emotional time so that they will not be forced to make decisions they might not be prepared to make. If a religious faith is an important part of your end-of-life concerns, make that clear in your plan.

Decide whether you want to have a traditional funeral and have your body buried in a cemetery; whether to be cremated and have a memorial service; whether to consider "green" burial options; or whether to donate your body for medical research and education. Perhaps you want to have your body preserved by freezing and kept indefinitely. Be specific to avoid confusion.

If you chose burial, a burial plot can be purchased and a mortuary contracted to carry out your funeral plan. Prepaid options relieve your loved ones of making urgent decisions and limits their financial obligations. You may also choose to be cremated, either by heat or by alkaline hydrolysis, and have your remains buried or scattered. Whatever you decide, it is important to discuss your thoughts and plans with those individuals who will be responsible for settling your affairs and carrying out your final wishes.

Consider charitable options as well. Organ or whole-body donations can be arranged through medical institutions such as medical schools. Most public and private medical schools will have bequest programs that support their research and education missions. When you register as a donor, you will receive a card to carry in your wallet or purse. In most programs the institution will pick up the body when death occurs, but there may be some geographic limitations. Most donated bodies are used for teaching anatomy to the next generation of healthcare workers including doctors, nurses, therapists, and morticians. The remains are often cremated and later returned to the family. Most schools currently have a yearly memorial service for the family and friends of the donors. Many of the students who had the privilege of learning from the anatomy bequests participate in the programs.

There are several less-used options available. You can request a natural burial where the body is shrouded or placed in a degradable pod and buried without embalming, casket, or vaults. Some mortuaries offer conservation memorial forests where ashes can be spread over a designated piece of land. You can choose more environmentally friendly chemical cremation using water and potassium hydroxide.

Spend time searching for the options available in your region. A traditional funeral and burial can be expensive. Make plans ahead to avoid your loved ones needing to make urgent decisions during an emotional time.

Organizing
Important
Papers

GETTING ORGANIZED

If you have read this whole book, you know you have a lot of personal information to collect and organize.

We should simplify and organize our records to make it easier to find what we need while we are alive and for our survivors when we are not. Designate agents for health (chapter 15) and set up a durable power of attorney for financial matters (chapter 25). These are two critical designations. You should select them now, if you have not already done so.

We will make some suggestions for organizing your information in this chapter. You may have already created a filing system that works for you. If so, it is wise to check your information against our recommendations and fill in any gaps.

EMERGENCY and GENERAL FILES

1. Names and contact information of family, friends, and organizations who should be notified if you are incapacitated or die

2. Medical information: major healthcare problems, healthcare directives, name and contact numbers for healthcare agent, primary medical-care contact, other medical providers if appropriate, Medicare/Medicaid card, Medicare supplement insurance information, any special orders regarding life-sustaining treatment such as a POLST order, Do Not Resuscitate/Intubate/Hospitalize orders, or contacts for body or organ donation, if designated

3. Personal information: birth and marriage certificates, divorce decrees, military records, passports, and previous addresses (which may be required for identification)

4. Financial records: wills and trusts, name and contact number
   for financial agent, life-insurance provider, accident insurance
   provider, list of death benefits, any annuity accounts and contact
   numbers, social security card and numbers, retirement-plan
   information, safety-deposit box location and key, bank and
   investment-account numbers and locations, credit card location
   and numbers, recent tax records (past three years recommended),
   outstanding debts including mortgages, any loans owed to you, real
   estate deeds and other documents, and a list of recurring monthly
   and annual payments, subscriptions, and account information

5. Personal property: car titles and licenses, property and other
   ownership documents

6. Personal advisors: names and contact information for
   lawyer(s), investment advisor(s), insurance agent, stockbroker,
   and accountant

7. Internet and account-user IDs and passwords list (Update every 3–4 months.)

8. Funeral or memorial arrangements, cremation plans, burial plots

9. Letters of instruction, memoirs, legacy letters, other information to pass on to heirs

Have all your pertinent information in one accessible place for another person to retrieve when needed. You could use this workbook to record and attach documents. Another option is to use a metal file box kept in a safe place. Don't expect to collect all your information and get it together in a few hours, unless your are already well organized. Depending on the current location of this information, it may take days or weeks to create a workable system. When complete, notify your family, healthcare representative, and financial agent.

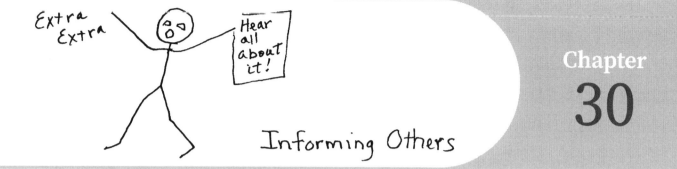

CONVERSATIONS THAT MATTER

Throughout this book we have encouraged readers to begin conversations about living and dying with their family and loved ones. They need to know your wishes and the thinking behind your decisions.

How should we have these important conversations? The younger generation may not wish to talk about end-of-life issues. There is no right way to have these discussions, but you need to have them. Accept that there may be family resistance and forge ahead with a plan.

When selecting your trusted healthcare agent it is important to have a one-to-one discussion about your wishes, clarify any questions, and gain their acceptance for the responsibility. Also make sure the agent has a copy of your healthcare directive, knows who has other copies, and where the original document is kept.

Have a similar discussion with your financial agent. That person or institution will have the legal authority to make financial decisions if you are incapacitated or no longer living. Again, the location of your financial records and safety deposit boxes should be clear and accessible.

Have a conversation with others who have an interest in your well-being and who will be affected by your death. Everyone concerned needs to understand your decision and wishes. Their willingness to carry out your wishes, even if they are not in full personal agreement, will give you peace of mind.

We introduced you to Fern and Arnie in previous chapters. They had informed their son and daughter that they planned to be buried in a family plot in a rural church cemetery near where they had grown up. They brought their son to the cemetery several times to where their parents and grandparents were buried over the last 100 years. They taught their son about cleaning the markers and planting summer flowers. As the years progressed, the father had more difficulty getting down to do the plantings and brought a folding chair to observe the annual ritual. They had contracted with a local monument company for markers. They were clear with their children about wanting a traditional casket burial. They had also prepaid the monument company for the inscription to be made when they died.

The conversations about their wishes and plans were stretched out over a period of years. There was plenty of time to clarify and answer questions their son or daughter might have. When Fern's husband died, he was buried and his marker was filled in. Fern lived several more years. She kept all her important papers in a metal file that was handled with care by her children when she was required to change residencies in her last years of life. When she died, she was buried next to her husband and her final date was engraved into her grave marker.

Ralph and Ramona were in their early seventies. Both had retired and were filling their new leisure time with travels and long-delayed hobbies and volunteer work. Their six children were largely successful and were no longer a major concern. They enjoyed their family get-togethers, which had grown to include over twenty individuals.

Ralph and Ramona had made many plans on how they wanted to spend their retirement. They decided to stay in the same area where they had raised their family and where most of them still lived. They took the trips they had postponed while they were working and felt good about the lives they were leading.

Then one of their close friends died suddenly. That family was unprepared and forced to make decisions on short notice without knowing what the deceased person wanted. Ralph and Ramona began thinking about how they wanted to end their lives and started making plans.

First they decided they didn't want to be a burden on their children or grandchildren. They decided they wanted to be cremated, have some of their ashes scattered in the river near their home and the remainder buried in a marked grave in a local cemetery. They knew some members of their family were more traditional and might object.

Ralph and Ramona's family gathered at Thanksgiving time. Ralph and Ramona asked the family to hear their plans as they approached the last years of their lives. As expected they started to get feedback and the family conversation began. By the time they gathered for Thanksgiving Ralph and Ramona had held individual discussions with several of their children. A granddaughter had said she didn't want them to talk about dying. During the weeks before Thanksgiving they asked their eldest son to be their healthcare and financial agent. He was an accountant for a medical-supply firm and they felt he would be well accepted by the rest of the family.

After dinner Ralph and Ramona had everyone sit down as they presented what they wanted and didn't want for health care, if they couldn't make their own decisions. They explained why they had chosen their son to lead any family discussion about their care. They hoped the family would agree with how they wished to limit care if there was little prospect of recovery.

Ralph and Ramona went on to tell them about their wills and their plan to divide any money or property remaining after the second person died equally among each child or the child's heirs. There was some discussion about not wanting to talk about their dying, but the family all agreed to honor their wishes.

Over the ensuing years there were continued conversations as the family members interacted. When Ramona died suddenly in her late eighties, the end-of-life plans went into effect. The family held a ceremony placing half of her ashes at her favorite spot in the river and the remainder in the local cemetery. When Ralph died in his early nineties his ashes were placed and celebrated in the same way.

These are just two examples of end-of-life planning. These families planned well and understood the value and peace of mind that can result when the conversations are open, honest, and accepted by all concerned. There are many events at the end of life that are not predictable, but there is much that can be done to assure the ending goes as well as possible.

This guidebook will not answer all the questions you might have about living well or all the decisions that you and your loved ones will need to make as your life draws to a close. The Conversations That Matter work group have used their experiences in selecting topics and organizing the content in one place. We hope you have found this guide useful. We are honored to have added to your thinking about living well and dying well.

SOURCES

Baines, Barry K. *Ethical Wills: Putting Your Values on Paper.* 2nd Ed. Boston, MA: Da Capo Lifelong Books, 2006.

Bateson, Mary Catherine. *Composing a Further Life: The Age of Active Wisdom.* New York, NY: Vintage, 2011.

Butler, Katy. *Knocking on Heaven's Door: The Path to a Better Way of Death.* New York, NY: Scribner, 2013.

Byock, Ira. *The Best Care Possible: A Physician's Quest to Transform Care Through the End of Life.* New York, NY: Avery Publishing, 2013.

Byock, Ira. *The Four Things That Matter Most.* New York, NY: Atria Books, 2014.

Casarett, David. *How to Chose a Hospice.* http://www.huffingtonpost .com/david-casarett-md/hospice_b_5517717.html

Chopra, Deepak. *Metahuman: Unleashing Your Infinite Potential.* New York, NY: Harmony Books, 2019.

Douglas, Sandra. *Anti-Aging by Choice: Easy Lifestyle Changes to Slow the Signs of Aging.* CreateSpace Independent Publishing Platform, 2012.

Emmons, Henry and Alter, David. *Staying Sharp: 9 Keys for a Youthful Brain Through Modern Science.* New York, NY: Atria Books, 2016.

Erickson, Karla. *How We Die Now: Intimacy and the Work of Dying.* Philadelphia, PA: Temple University Press, 2013.

Freed, Rachael. *Your Legacy Matters: A Multi-Generational Guide for Writing your Ethical Will.* Minerva Press, 2013.

Gawande, Atul. *Being Mortal: Medicine and What Happens in the End.* New York, NY: Metropolitan Books, 2014.

Goodman, Ellen. *A Conversation-Starter Kit.* Institute for Healthcare Improvement, 2021. https://www.ihi.org/engage/initiatives/conversationproject

Hickman, Martha W. *Healing After Loss: Daily Meditations for Working Through Grief.* New York, NY: William Morrow, 1994.

Jenkinson, Stephen. *Come of Age: The Case for Elderhood in a Time of Trouble.* Berkeley, CA: North Atlantic Books, 2018.

Jenkinson, Stephen. *Die Wise: A Manifesto for Sanity and Soul.* Berkeley, CA: North Atlantic Books, 2018.

Kalinithi, Paul. *When Breath Becomes Air.* New York, NY: Random House, 2016.

Lee, Barbara Coombs. *Finish Strong: Putting your Priorities First at Life's End.* Compassion & Choices, 2018. https://compassionandchoices.org/finish-strong/

Leider, Richard and Shapiro, David. *Claiming Your Place at the Fire: Living the Second Half of your Life on Purpose.* Oakland, CA: Berrett & Kochler Publishers, 2004.

Levine, Stephen and Levine, Ondrea. *Who Dies: An Investigation of Conscious Living and Dying.* New York, NY: Anchor Books, 1989.

Mace, Nancy L. and Rabins, Peter V. *The 36-Hour Day: A Family Guide to Caring for People Who Have Alzheimer Disease, Related Dementias, and Memory Loss.* Baltimore, MD: Johns Hopkins Press, 2017.

Minnesota Attorney General, The Office of. *Probate and Planning: A Guide to Planning for the Future.* 445 Minnesota Street, Suite 1400, St. Paul, MN 55101, 651-296-3353, 800-657-3529.

Mitford, Jessica. *The American Way of Death.* New York, NY: Simon & Schuster, 1963.

Neumann, Ann. *The Good Death: An Exploration of Dying in America.* Boston, MA: Beacon Press, 2017.

Nuland, Sherwin B. *The Art of Aging: A Doctor's Prescription for Well-Being.* New York, NY: Random House, 2008.

Nuland, Sherwin B. *How We Die: Reflections on Life's Final Chapter.* New York, NY: Vintage, 1995.

Peter Pauper Press. *I'm Dead, Now What? Important Information About My Belongings, Business Affairs, and Wishes.* Hawthorne, NY: Peter Pauper Press, 2015.

Reed, William G. *Lessons from a Disabled Caregiver: Thriving Together and Maintaining Independence with Physical Disability and Dementia.* Jefferson, NC: Toplight Books, 2021.

Sacks, Oliver. *Gratitude.* New York, NY: Knopf, 2015.